A remembrance of
our trip to New England
in September of 1991.

BOSTON IN COLOR

BOSTON
in Color

A Collection of Color

Photographs by

PETER H. DREYER

With Text and

Notes on the Illustrations by

STEWART DILL McBRIDE

HASTINGS HOUSE · PUBLISHERS

New York, 10016

PUBLISHED 1977 BY HASTINGS HOUSE, PUBLISHERS,INC.

Reprinted February, 1979

Reprinted April, 1980

Reprinted August, 1984

Reprinted January, 1986

Library of Congress Cataloging in Publication Data

McBride, Stewart Dill.
 Boston in color.

 (Profiles of America)
  1. Boston—Description—1951–   2. Boston—
Description—1951–   —Views. I. Dreyer, Peter H.
II. Title.
F73.52.M32 1976   974.4'61'04   76-44540
ISBN 0-8038-0775-9

Printed in Shen Zhen, China

CONTENTS

The Two-Legged Town

I

"SUCCESS TO the Crooked But interesting TOWN OF BOSTON!" So reads the inscription on a jug once ordered from Liverpool by a Boston ship captain. Today that historic piece of pottery rests in Boston's Old State House, and a careless or vindictive historian might presume the jug to be early evidence of Boston's graft. The presumption would be mistaken: the seaman's word "crooked" referred to the roads, not to the people. Boston's Puritan settlers found it easier to stick to the straight and narrow in their halls of worship than on their twisted highways.

Colonial legend holds that Boston's first city planners were cows—not sacred cows; just cows. It was the gentle animals' whim to wander. On their way to the Common's tender grass they wended around many a cove, marsh, and steep hill on the rocky peninsula where their Puritan masters had chosen to settle in 1630. The colonists, following the trailblazing cattle rather than cutting their own paths, thus let the animals dictate a tortuous street pattern— that labyrinth of irrational one-way streets which so frustrate Boston drivers today.

The cows also got their way on colonial Beacon Hill, where colonial building codes required that passageways between houses be wide enough to admit a cow, and high enough for a boy with a basket on his head. We have cattle to thank for the Boston Common, that forty-five-acre downtown pasture which today offers secretaries and shoppers a lawn on which to spread their brown bagged lunches, a "Brimstone Corner" for soapbox orators and saffron-robed Buddhists, and a wading pool adorned (in summer) with bare-bottomed babies.

7

First surveyed by four-legged creatures, Boston is a two-legged town. It was built for pedestrians, and the best touring example comes from Paul Revere's horse: hoof it. Downtown's beguiling nooks and alleys, cobblestones, polished brass door knockers, and manicured gardens were never meant to be framed in the windshield of a passing automobile. Boston's heart and soul are best understood at a leisurely saunter that is impossible on any set of wheels but roller skates.

The city's history and architecture are etched with details too intriguing to drive past. Even the veteran Bostonian, who may have hiked the Freedom Trail with umpteen sets of cousins from Cleveland, is in for some surprises. How many know that, in the posh Parker House where Ralph Waldo Emerson convened his famous Saturday Club of intellectuals, both Ho Chi Minh and Malcolm X worked as waiters—though not at the same time? Who recalls that at 12 Tyler Street in Boston's Chinatown, Sun Yat-sen once plotted with half a dozen Chinese refugees to overthrow the Manchu Dynasty?

Boston has the credentials Lewis Mumford demanded of a great city: hills, water, and "great variety within a small room." The town is not a checkerboard of concrete canyons, but a chameleon of contrasts whose appearance changes dramatically with temperamental weather or a short walk. Boston is of cosmopolitan size, yet its buildings are on a human European scale which tends to keep the city "livable," and prevents people from feeling lost.

Yet in Boston, getting "lost" is a probable adventure. On arriving here Arnold Bennett wrote: "I usually go about strange places with a map, but I found the map of Boston even more complex than the city it sought to explain. If I did not lose myself, it was because I never trusted myself alone; other people lost me."

Compounding the intrigue of navigating downtown Boston is its mystery of place names. In his delightful book, *Boston Ways: High, By and Folk*, George F. Weston, Jr. notes that the geographical center of the city is Roxbury. To the north of Roxbury is the South End, not to be mistaken for South Boston which lies due east of the South End. To the north of South Boston lies East Boston, and to the southwest of that is the North End.

If you're trying to find your way to Old North Church, or to Old Ironsides, to the North End's Italian pastries and cherrystone clams, or to the short-ribs and short-tempered waitresses in the Durgin-Park dining rooms—ask the assistance of a native. Bostonians are friendly folks—friendlier than most people give them credit for—though their speech is something less than euphonious to the untrained ear.

8

Bostonese, a dialect which gained notoriety while Kennedy inhabited the White House, is an exotic hybrid of Irish, Brahmin, Downeast Yankee, and a tad of Brooklyn nasal (which varies in strength with one's socio-economic class). R's are mysteriously and consistently dropped, so that "park" becomes "pahk" (as in "Pahk yah cah in Hahvud Yahd"); "Bah Hahbah" is that posh Maine port where the bluebloods take their summer vacation; and rooms which sell liquor are pronounced like the sound a sheep is supposed to make. For no locutional logic, one must order a "frappe" to get ice cream in a milk shake. "Tonic" is the name given to the beverage known universally as soda pop.Boston's most famous fish is spelled three different ways on restaurant menus: scrod, schrod, shrode.

Adding to the difficulties of the Boston accent is a specialized vocabulary which evolved in the city's patchwork of ethnic villages, where the same word can get you a smile or a frown, depending on the neighborhood. Berlitz has no crash course for explorers visiting Boston, so here are a few words you'll find in the city but not in Webster's: fried matter (donut), dorm toolie (hard working MIT student), bunny holes (a game of marbles), whiffles (short haircuts), Irish Riviera (South Shore suburbs), rubber ground (asphalt), and soft as a sneakersfull (wishy washy). A "smoky Sou'wester" is a storm, not an Arizona fireman. If you're invited to the "fish tank," bring a chess board rather than a swimsuit. And don't forget that "peat from the same bog" is not an insult but an endearment.

Oliver Wendell Holmes, in one of his frequent and generous tributes to this city, described the Bostonian as, "...of almost pure and unmixed English blood; he is a proud squire, unmellowed, exacerbated and aestheticized by change of climate; ...[he] is simply an Americanized Englishman. As the Englishman is the physical bully of the world, so the Bostonian is the aesthetic and intellectual bully of America."

Indeed, many held Boston to be as English as the muffin—an admission that was revoltingly un-Revolutionary. It was a port town, whose higgledy-piggledy roads, tree-lined courts, and elegant town houses put the visiting Briton back in the Kensington of Georgian London.

Boston was never satisfied to be just another American downtown; it will always be that "city set on a hill" which cannot be hidden and does not choose to be. It is unlikely to acquire the glittering sprawl of a Houston or Los Angeles. It may never muster the drive and intensity of New York, nor the fastidious frontier femininity of a San Francisco, nor the brash bustle that surges through a Chicago. It doesn't have Pittsburgh's steel mills or Detroit's assembly lines. Here industry (finance, insurance, education, medicine) is clean—with the possible exception of that other big business, government. (Boston is one of the few big U.S. cities which is also a state capital.) There is nothing glamorous or frilly about Boston and her people. The city shoulders the understated elegance of a worn Burberry tweed coat. Boston, it seems, will always be herself, just plain respectable Boston.

But what *is* Boston? Ask those who spent some time here. Ralph Waldo Emerson wrote: "This town of Boston has a history. It is not an accident, not a windmill, or a railroad station, or a cross-roads tavern, or an army barracks grown up by time and luck to a place of wealth; but a seat of humanity, of men of principle, obeying a sentiment and marching loyally whither that should lead them; so that its annals are great historical lines, inextricably national, part of the history of political liberty."

"I remember Boston as a quiet effect," recalls H.G. Wells, "as something a little withdrawn, as a place standing aside from the throbbing interchange of East and West...I think of rows of well-built brown and ruddy homes, each with a certain sound architectural distinction, each with its two squares of neatly trimmed grass between itself and the broad quiet street, and each with its family of cultured people within...I recall the finished informality of the high tea. It is incredible how many people in Boston have selected her for their aesthetic symbol and expression."

Equally moved was muckraking journalist Lincoln Steffens: "I hate Boston. I don't know why. The people there are awfully good to me. But the general spirit is so far, far, far, back that it gets on my nerves...Boston has carried the practice of hypocrisy to the nth degree of refinement, grace and failure."

The debate continues. Both sides find themselves describing the city in superlatives. Whatever conclusion an outsider may draw, hardy-humble Boston always seems to have the last word. "Boston has earned its good name, and as for the unkind things that were said about it, one usually found some Boston man who said them first and better," penned Van Wyck Brooks.

What is Boston? Is it the Beacon Hill ancient from a Henry James novel, who carries a copy of his family tree to prove his ancestors arrived with the Puritans, aboard the "Arabella?" Is it the snobbish city where books were banned, and Back Bay's old guard rigidly walks a daily triangle between Beacon Street, State Street and the Somerset Club? Is Boston composed of Bibles, Brahmins or bosses? Is it an Irish cop from Southie (South Boston) who was "born on A Street, brought up on B Street," and swims year round in the icy Atlantic with his buddies at the L Street Bath House? Is it the blood-thirsty screams of Boston Bruin hockey fans, or genteel huzzahs at a Harvard

Club squash tournament? Is it Bulfinch's red brick "toothpick colonial" mansions, or Dorchester's wooden triple deckers? Is it clean living and dirty politics? Is Boston religious or irreverent? Eccentric or traditional?

The question, "What is Boston?" is becoming so difficult that one can no longer rely on the once dependable ditty:

> "And this is good old Boston,
> The home of the bean and the cod,
> Where the Lowells talk to the Cabots
> And the Cabots talk only to God."

Cod were once so abundant in New England waters that they became Massachusetts' state symbol. Today they are an endangered species. A good cup of chowder is hard to find, and those legendary legumes, Boston baked beans, are anticlimactic. The Lowells (frequently confused in the public mind with the Lodges) and the Cabots—like most of those Anglo-Saxon dynasties in the Social Register—have taken their talents and tax dollars to the suburbs. As for God, well, modern Bostonians know that no one—or everyone—has a direct line to Him; and to prove it the city harbors a rainbow of religions and untold private cults.

But food, family, and eternity are not the only Boston preoccupations. There is also politics—that unpredictable city institution. It was Boston which allowed Paul Revere to own eight slaves; where abolitionist William Lloyd Garrison was nearly lynched; and here, more recently, white neighborhoods have vehemently (and violently) resisted school desegregation. Yet this same city helped send the nation's only Black U.S. Senator (since post-Civil War Reconstruction) to Washington. His name is Edward Brooke.

The "Cradle of Liberty" is still rocking from the 1972 Presidential election: Massachusetts was the only state whose majority did not re-elect Richard Nixon. With characteristic swagger, Bostonians never let the other 49 states forget it. For several years they boasted from their bumper stickers: "We told you so," "Lone Star State," and "Nixon, 49; America, 1."

What *is* Boston? Visitors who decide to discover the town for themselves are usually happiest with their answers to this elusive question. But where should they begin? With a sightseeing bus? With a bird's eye view of the old city from the top of its newest skyscrapers? Should they ride the subway and simulate the cramped condition of the Pilgrims crossing on the Mayflower?

When examining the genesis of a town that originated as a "Bible Commonwealth", it is only proper, in the best Bostonian sense, to start: "In the beginning..."

II

"THE BEGINNING" of Boston predates even its founding in 1630, according to George Weston. It goes back to the days of olde when King Arthur was issuing those exclusive invitations to his Round Table. At that time, on the coast of Lincolnshire, England, there lived a wandering Saxon monk who would rather pray for fishermen than for princes; hence the unselfish monk was dubbed "The Boat Helper" (in Anglo-Saxon, "Bot-holph"). He was later canonized a seafarers' saint, and the coastal village where he founded a monastery in A.D. 654, was given the name St. Botolph's Town.

As with most good things, the name of the town wore down with use. Over the years, townspeople dropped a consonant here and a consonant there; St. Botolph's Town became Bottleston, Botolston, Buston, and finally Boston. (St. Botolph might shudder in his sandals to know this shorthand title given to his hometown. But he would withdraw his name from the calendar altogether were he to learn that St. Botolph's Street in Boston (Massachusetts) is today best known for its ladies of the night and a mushroom shaped restaurant which serves neither roast beef nor Yorkshire pudding, but quiche and coq au vin.)

Britain's Boston, it is said, furnished more worthy citizens for the original colonizing of America than did any other part of England. It was in Boston (England) in 1607, thirteen years before the Mayflower set sail, that the Pilgrim Fathers were jailed for trying to escape religious persecution. Attempting to flee to Holland, they were betrayed in Boston's port by a Dutch vessel master who had promised to ferry them to Amsterdam. After a few months in the English Boston's cramped cells, many of the Pilgrims were released, made their way to Holland, and formed the nucleus of those who sailed with Miles Standish on the Mayflower in 1620.

The Pilgrims led the way to New England, but they did not found Boston; a group of Calvinist zealots did that. Ten years after the Mayflower landed in the New World, 700 religious dissenters (many of them English Bostonians) calling themselves Puritans—they were trying to "purify" the Church of England—decided to put the Atlantic between themselves and their repressive king, Charles I. They were led by a Puritan lawyer named John Winthrop.

Winthrop's ship, the "Arabella," landed first in Salem, which the Puritans soon deserted for Charlestown. Across the river from Charlestown was the Shawmut Peninsula (presently downtown Boston), inhabited by friendly Indians. There also lived one not-so-friendly Englishman, who had originally come as a New World missionary of the Church of England. Rev. William Blackstone led a reclusive but happy existence on a fertile plot of land with a

200-volume library, herd of goats, and rose garden. He distinctly preferred trading oysters with the Indians to trading conversation with his fellow countrymen.

Initially the Puritans had little reason to be attracted by either Blackstone's farm animals or his reading material. They were put off, to say the least, by the hermit's insistence on wearing his "old canonical gown" in the woods. But because the brackish water in Charlestown was felling the Puritans at an alarming rate, Blackstone did have a single redeeming quality in the eyes of the thirsty settlers: he lived next to one of the best fresh water streams for miles. When the Anglican divine finally invited the newcomers to his peninsula, he soon realized his mistake. They graciously accepted his offer—every last one of them.

The Puritans wasted no time in naming the Shawmut Peninsula after their Boston hometown in Lincolnshire; and with characteristic Yankee generosity they "gave" Blackstone forty-five acres of his own property. Startled by such an overnight population explosion, Blackstone decided it was time to move on. He packed his belongings on a brindled bull (which he rode "for want of a horse"), and headed for Rhode Island. Before he left, the colonists chipped in six shillings apiece (amounting to about $150) to buy Blackstone's forty-five acres; and they turned the lot into "Common" property for the "feeding of cattel" and a "place for a trayning field."

Boston's Common remains the oldest public park in America. A few Boston purists claim ancestral rights to graze hypothetical herds; but the animals that frolic here nowadays are not cows but canines—some, perhaps, pedigree descendants of that single pup who accompanied the Puritans in 1630.

One of Winthrop's first acts as governor of this "Bible Commonwealth" (where every voter had to be a church member) was to erect stocks on the Common. Ironically, the carpenter who built them was the first to have his ankles sample his handiwork; Winthrop claimed he charged too much. Similar rewards were given to anyone found eavesdropping, meddling, pulling hair, pushing his wife, "selling dear," "selling strong water by small measure," "sleeping in meeting," or "dissenting from the rest of the jury." Mothers were not permitted to caress their children on Sunday. One sea captain was whipped for kissing his wife in public, and a year later he was lashed again for neglecting her. It was hard to win.

Boston's time-honored provincialism is no doubt a partial holdover from these founding Puritans' simple manners, primitiveness, and rustic philosophy cultivated in this culturally isolated "state of nature." In the Puritan theology of "thou shalt nots," the theater was considered wicked, and as late as 1750 it was banned by a legislative edict. Curiously enough, stage-plays were introduced in Boston in 1775 by the British, who tried to cheer up their soldiers with Shakespeare during the city's occupation. When Washington forced the British to evacuate Boston in March 1776, he also expelled the city's brief theatrical tradition, which took another decade to resurrect itself.

Disdain for drama belonged to the same strain of Puritanism that lay behind the 20th century "banned in Boston" campaign. This was launched by the Watch and Ward Society, which closed the gates of the city to the literary likes of James Joyce's *Ulysses*, Eugene O'Neil's *Strange Interlude*, Upton Sinclair's *Oil*, and the works of Sean O'Casey.

In modern day Boston, the official attitude toward sin has soured. The present day city fathers have drawn boundaries around a less-than-Puritan downtown honky-tonk area dubbed the "Combat Zone," and reclassified it the "adult entertainment district." Where else but in Boston can you still find citizens who consider nude statuary "indecent?" Where else but in the Combat Zone would you find a burlesque house named "The Pilgrim," and a porno shop called the "Mayflower?" What would the Puritans have said about that?

III

"THE TOPOGRAPHY of Boston has undergone greater changes at the hand of man than any other city, ancient or modern," declares the Encyclopedia Britannica. Unlike San Franciscans, who worship their terrain, the people of Boston have always manhandled their topography. Conversely, New England's rugged landscape has resisted and decidedly shaped the self-reliant character of Boston—that "state of mind almost entirely surrounded by water."

Boston's tailor-made port became the city's purse. Settlers reaped their prosperity from the fertile sea, not from the rocky New England soil. With an unlimited demand for fish in Catholic Europe, New England merchants became the pipeline for shipping dried cod to overseas customers. Boston had also evolved into a vital link in the "triangle trade" of rum, slaves and molasses, with West Africa and the West Indies. By 1700, the Massachusetts colony was booming; its fleet was the third largest in the English-speaking world: Boston claimed to be the biggest town in British North America.

It didn't take long for this increasingly independent plum of prosperity to catch the eye of the British King, who decided it was time to haul in the royal reins. In 1686 the Crown cancelled the Massachusetts Bay Colony's charter and appointed a royal governor. A few generations later the British army and navy came to the aid of the colonists to eliminate the "French menace" in

Canada. The Seven Years' War ended in 1763, and English aristocracy felt it only just that the Americans (who after all had benefited most) help foot the bill for the war. Bostonians had smuggled their way around earlier British unpopular taxes, so this time the King imposed a tough series of revenue measures: the Sugar Act of 1764, the Stamp Acts of 1765, and the Townshend Act of 1767.

In hopes of bailing out its faltering East India Company, Britain attempted in 1773 to unload in Boston a surplus of taxed tea. Outraged by "monopolization" of trade on this popular drink, the town refused to unload the new tea shipment. The famous Boston Tea Party occurred in December: some 60 patriots, disguised as Mohawk Indians, tossed 342 chests of tea from the ship into the harbor. The British Prime Minister Lord North, retaliated by closing the port of Boston, and appointed as governor General Thomas Gage, commander of the British troops.

Between 1770 and 1775, the population of Boston fell from 20,000 to 3,000 as patriots headed for the hills to set up their "government in exile" and train the Minutemen militia. On April 18, 1775, Gage sent out an evening raiding party to capture rebel ammunition supplies hidden in Concord, seventeen miles from Boston. The raiders' departure from Boston was noted. Two warning lanterns hung in the Old North Church steeple, signalled Paul Revere and William Dawes (the midnight rider who didn't make it into Longfellow's famous poem) to gallop into the darkness. The riders stayed a few hoofbeats ahead of the British, and spread word through the slumbering countryside that redcoats were marching toward Lexington and Concord.

The King's soldiers confronted the alerted militia on the "rude bridge" over the Concord River, and fired that "shot heard 'round the world." The redcoats retreated to Boston and tended to their wounded—more injured pride than injured soldiers—as some 16,000 colonial militiamen ringed the city. So began the eleven-month siege, highlighted on June 17 by the Battle of Bunker Hill—which really was fought on Charlestown's nearby Breed's Hill.

On July 1, General Washington came from Philadelphia to take command of the newborn Continental Army, which proceeded to bottle up Boston. With the help of the cannons which General Henry Knox dragged from New York's Fort Ticonderoga and Crown Point during the winter of 1775–76, General Washington fortified Dorchester Heights. From there he stared down the British ships in the harbor, and forced them to evacuate the city. They sailed for Halifax on March 17, 1776. The Revolution went elsewhere—New York, Philadelphia, Morristown, Saratoga and finally Yorktown, where Cornwallis surrendered on Oct. 19, 1781.

Major wars are usually followed by a hiatus for reconstruction. Boston, after the War of Independence, had some fancy fiscal footwork to perform. The city faced economic depression, staggering unemployment, and galloping inflation—prices jumped 200 percent between 1775 and 1780. The city could no longer rely on trade with a mother country, and was forced to find new and more remote customers. As usual, however, New England ingenuity prevailed. Boston sea captains headed for China, India, Java, and the Pacific Northwest. The China trade was particularly profitable, and was largely responsible for Boston's vast wealth during the Federal period. Between 1789 and 1810, Massachusetts' fishing and merchant fleets increased ten-fold, and the Loyalist merchants, who had dominated commerce before the revolution, were soon replaced by the new "Codfish Aristocracy" of men with names like Cabot, Lowell, Otis and Hancock. As John Singleton Copley had painted colonial worthies such as Paul Revere, so Gilbert Stuart painted portraits of Boston's new patricians. Red-brick mansions, designed by architect Charles Bulfinch, were testimonies to the influence and affluence of Federalist aristocracy.

Colonial Boston, devoted to taming new lands and fighting the British, spared little time for elegant architecture. The peace and prosperity of Federalist Boston was a more leisurely setting. Bulfinch—architectural genuis, city planner, founder of Boston's first real estate development firm, and chairman of the Board of Selectmen—wielded the power of a modern mayor and left a signature on the city as distinct as that of Christopher Wren's on London. In 1795 he crowned Beacon Hill with the grand neo-classical Massachusetts State House. Soon all of "the Hill's" pastures and blueberry fields were covered with his red-brick rowhouses, granite Greek revival mansions, and streets of cobblestone. But Bulfinch, despite being a Yankee blueblood, faced his own rocky roads. In 1793 he was working in the fleetingly fashionable South End, on the Tontine Crescent (modelled after the Crescents in Bath, England). The project went bankrupt, and justice proved to be no respecter of rank. America's most famous architect was jailed for non-payment.

IV

JOHN LOWELL, Jr., founder of the Lowell Institute, wrote in 1832, "The prosperity of my native land, New England, which is sterile and unproductive, must depend hereafter, as it has heretofore depended, on the moral qualities, and secondly on the intelligence of the inhabitant." Amid the rigors of 19th century New England, necessity indeed was adopting, if not mothering, Yankee invention in Boston.

Elevators, incandescent lamps, phonographs, typewriters, carpet sweepers, bustle seats were becoming a new part of daily life. Back porch inventors were patenting the compleat clothespin, the ultimate mousetrap, and those Rube Goldberg flying machines which never did quite get off the ground.

In Boston a travelling salesman named King Camp Gillette dreamed up the safety razor. Soon Americans were trading beards for 5 o'clock shadows, and streetcar conductors could no longer issue tickets which identified passengers by the style of their whiskers. Alexander Graham Bell, teacher of the deaf, taught the telegraph to "talk" in his attic workshop at 109 Court Street in Boston, and eventually shrank the world to an electronic village. George Grant, a black Harvard student, patented a calculating machine that was 8 feet long, had over 15,000 parts, and cost more than $10,000. Yet he will most likely be remembered for his contraption of leisure—the golf tee.

Boston, however, profited most from the less glamorous gadgets; the Boston-designed sewing machine, coupled with the power loom imported from Lancashire, England, ushered the industrial revolution into the Hub. Smokestacks became status symbols. Waterfalls and rivers were harnessed to convert leather into shoes and cotton into waistcoats. As Boston's own tidal power (from the milldam built across the Back Bay) proved insufficient, mill towns soon sprang up in northern Massachusetts and New Hampshire along the Merrimack River like fiddleheads in spring. They were named after the men who founded them—Francis Cabot Lowell and Abbott Lawrence. Machines transformed the port of Boston into a booming East Coast manufacturing center.

One resource that burgeoning Boston lacked was a large labor force. A potato famine 3,000 miles away, however, was to solve that problem. By mid-19th century, Boston's trinity of growth was complete: invention, industry, and immigrants—Irish immigrants.

They traded potato rot and starvation in Western Ireland for squalor in Boston. They came to Boston expecting a "Promised Land" where the streets were paved with gold; they discovered many of the city's streets were not paved at all, and they were hired to pave them. They sweated fifteen-hour days, constructing highways and railroads, painting houses, gardening, for a few pennies an hour. Boston's growth, paid for from the breast pocket of the Brahmin, was built on the back of the immigrant.

These newcomers ignited a population explosion in Boston, the likes of which the city will probably never see again. Between 1800 and 1900, the number of city residents had multiplied nearly thirty times, to 560,000—a few thousand shy of the modern day population. At the height of 19th century immigration, the density of people in the North End was said to be exceeded only by that of Calcutta.

The arrival of the immigrants had also altered the city's religious base. The Puritan settlement had become a Catholic town. Forbidden in the early colonial days, Catholic churches numbered twenty-eight by 1875. Boston's Irish-Americans today remain by far the city's biggest ethnic group (nearly 190,000 persons—more than the combined population of Limerick and Cork counties in Ireland).

Friction between Catholics and Protestants further heightened the fear among many unskilled Yankee laborers that the hyphenated Americans would steal their jobs. Storefronts broke out in signs which read: "Help Wanted: No Irish Need Apply." The bigotry crested in the nativist, anti-Catholic "Know-Nothing" movement and exploded with the mob burning of Charles-town's Ursuline Convent in 1834.

In the 1880s a second wave of immigrants (from Southern and Eastern Europe) not only added to the Catholic strength but precipitated an internecine church struggle between the Irish, Italians and Poles. The new influx of immigrants, however, has the unanticipated effect of distracting Brahmin prejudice from the Irish. The Yankees were forced to concede that at least the Irish spoke English—after a fashion.

A handful of St. Patrick's people did escape from the ghettos into affluent enclaves of "Lace Curtain Irish." Mayor John Fitzgerald, among the Irish *nouveaux riches*, threw a posh "coming-out" party in 1911 for his daughter, Rose Fitzgerald (who later married a first generation Irish-American, Joseph Kennedy, and mothered a United States President and two U.S. Senators.) Fitzgerald, and most of Boston's Irish, however, realized they would never be admitted into the front ranks of high caste Brahmin society. While the Irish half of the population was unable to gain entrance to the boardrooms, private clubs, and parlors, by the turn of the century it had come to dominate City Hall and the civil service. The Brahmins owned Boston, but the Irish ran it.

Hugh O'Brien was elected the city's first foreign-born mayor in 1884, and began a political tradition of Boston Irish politics that has been echoed throughout the subsequent history of the city and the nation with Celtic names such as John W. McCormack, former Speaker of the U.S. House of Representatives, Thomas P. "Tip" O'Neill, House majority leader, as well as those of the Kennedy clan. (Between the 1910 election of John Fitzgerald and today, Boston has had only two mayors who were not of Irish descent.)

In the pre-Social Security era, men like Martin Lomasney, the greatest of Boston's bosses, built political czardoms on a self-serving, ward-heeling brand of "black jack democracy" devoted to easing the plight of the immigrant. This usually meant finding him clothes, job, housing—and instructions on where and *how* to vote: Democrat, of course. Lomasney ruled the West End; Patrick Joseph Kennedy dominated East Boston. John F. Kennedy's other grandfather, John F. Fitzgerald (who was nicknamed "Honey Fitz" after wooing the ladies at a political rally with a honey-voiced rendition of "Sweet Adeline") was the unquestioned king of the North End. In Boston's South End, James Michael Curley, son of an Irish hod carrier, got his political start and went on to rule all of Boston as mayor. Today he is immortalized as the fictional Frank Skeffington in Edwin O'Connor's, *The Last Hurrah.*

Vote "early and often for Curley" was the success slogan of this Gaelic Robin Hood, who was once jailed for sixty days (during which time he was elected city alderman). He had been convicted of taking a civil service exam for a less capable constituent. Curley's last term as mayor was interrupted by another five-month stint as an inmate—this time in Danbury, Conn. federal prison, under the charge that he'd used the U.S. mail to defraud.

He was cunning, reckless, eloquent and vindictive; but perhaps his political style is best remembered for its resilience. He lost more mayoral elections that he won. Nevertheless, his was a remarkable political career at that. It included sixteen years off and on as mayor of Boston (four terms in all), a term as Massachusetts governor during the Depression, four terms in the U.S. Congress, one term as state representative, and the one-time chairmanship of the Puerto Rico delegation to the 1936 Democratic convention. Despite his rambunctious political manners, "Gentlemen Jim" was known as a man who got things done—which was more than one could say for the "Goo-Goos" (good government reformers) whose highminded rhetoric meant little to the impoverished immigrant.

Working class politics was Boston's number one sport in the late 19th century, but athletics trailed only a close second. John L. Sullivan, Boston born and bred, was the unlikely offspring of a 5'3" father and an 180 pound mother. Preferring punching to preaching (the career chosen for him by his parents), young Sullivan quickly became known in the club boxing circuit as "Boston's Hercules." In 1882, during a bare-knuckled boxing match in Mississippi, "John L." KO'd defending champ Paddy Ryan with a ninth round right-hander which Ryan later said felt like "a telegraph pole shoved against me endways." For the next decade Sullivan ruled the ring. (Boston boys Jack Sharkey and Rocky Marciano were soon to follow in his footwork.) As notorious for his boozing as for his boxing, Sully turned teetotaler in 1905, and travelled the country preaching the virtues of temperance.

19

The "National Game"—baseball—goes back to the mid-19th century, and was popularized in Boston by the likes of a young pitcher named George Herman Ruth (more commonly known as "Babe"). Until the "miracle" Braves moved to Milwaukee in 1949, Boston boasted teams in both baseball leagues—the National, and the American (represented by Boston's Red Sox, who won the first World Series against Pittsburgh in 1903). Babe Ruth, Ted Williams, Hugh Duffy and Mike "King" Kelly are indelibly part of the lore in this "City of Champions" where, each spring, its fanatic fans are stung by "Fenway Fever."

The fans in this sports-crazy town know more about the players than do the team managers, and there is no sporting event in Boston which involves more spectators or more enthusiasm than the grueling twenty-six-mile footrace, the world-famous Boston Marathon—a tradition dating from 1897. Every Patriots' Day, after the city pays tribute to the midnight ride of Paul Revere and William Dawes, a blister brigade of more than 2,000 runners from around the world takes position behind a white line in the tiny suburban town of Hopkinton. This athletic army—lawyers and firemen, grade schoolers and grandfathers—stretches the length of two football fields. Helicopters hover overhead, state police rev their motorcycles; and at high noon, with the blast of the Brown family's traditional starting gun, the dam of humanity bursts—unleashing a sea of bobbing heads, flying pigtails, baseball caps and gritting teeth.

What does the winner gain from such heroic labor? Perhaps only the cheers, the traditional bowl of beef stew (awarded to each finisher), and a laurel wreath for the sweaty brow. Runners continue to stagger across the yellow finish line at the downtown Prudential Center until dusk. In this ultimate of amateur athletic events, all finishers are conquerors, if not winners.

That's Boston.

V

"ALL I claim for Boston is that it is the thinking centre of the continent, and therefore of the planet," wrote Oliver Wendell Holmes—a man not unduly enamored with himself and his Boston. During Boston's Victorian Gilded Age, this "Autocrat of the Breakfast Table," christened the city "The Hub of the Universe." (Most post-Civil War Boston residents conceded, with Ptolemaic humility, that their city was only the "Hub of the Solar System"). It was the same modest Oliver Wendell Holmes ("properly" adorned with a trinity of names) who popularized the expression "Boston Brahmin," referring to the city's social elite "with their houses by Bulfinch, their monopoly of Beacon Street, their ancestral portraits and Chinese porcelain, humanitarianism, Unitarian faith in the march of mind, Yankee shrewdness and New England exclusiveness."

Holmes well understood the Anglo-Saxon caste of which he was a firm and fashionable pillar. He accurately reflected the self-confidence of Victorian Boston, the thirty-five year period between the Civil War and the turn of the century. William Dean Howells, a midwest author drawn to this center of light and learning, remarked of Boston during that period: "She would rather perish by fire and sword than be suspected of vulgarity; a critical, fastidious Boston, dissatisfied with the rest of the hemisphere."

Oddly enough, many of our impressions of Boston today were physically and mentally molded during the city's high noon when, fed by post-Civil War peace and prosperity, the Hub expanded in body and mind. When Johnny came marching home from Gettysburg he found downtown Boston bursting with immigrants and industry which could no longer be contained on the pear-shaped Shawmut Peninsula. The city's humble hills, once a source of beauty, became a source of building stone and landfill. Throughout the 19th century, hilltops were shoveled into the surrounding marshes, bays and salt flats to make room for new residences and factories. The Roxbury Neck, narrow enough in colonial days to be entirely submerged at high tide, was raised and widened to create Boston's South End. Here high-stooped, bowfronted brownstone and brick townhouses, with mansard roofs, were set on tree-shaded squares; they gave the South End distinct London charm and a fleeting mid-century modishness. The Back Bay, however, was about to steal the architectural show.

Beginning in 1857 gravel was hauled nine miles by train to fill in 450 acres of tidal salt flats on the Charles River, "out back" of the city. This "Back Bay" had been cut off from cleansing ocean tides (a milldam had blocked it in 1821); and it had become a stinking cesspool of city sewage and waste. At the request of the City Health Department, and in the interest of urban expansion, 80 men and 145 railroad cars were employed round the clock. They unloaded gravel for the next forty-three years, and recovered an area from downtown Boston to the present Kenmore Square.

Street layout of the Back Bay's "new land" was not left up to wandering cows this time. Arthur Gilman, the appointed landscape architect, was inspired by the spacious, well-ordered designs of the French Second Empire." Wrote a visiting Briton after viewing the "new land": "The inscrutable, the unknowable Back Bay...is evidence of a society in equilibrium, and therefore

21

of a society which will receive genuinely new ideas with an extreme, if polite, caution, while welcoming with warm suavity old ideas that disguise themselves as novelties. It was a tremendous feat to reclaim from ooze the foundation of Back Bay." Thanks to novelist John P. Marquand, one can vividly picture patricians like the late George Apley, strolling by the buffed brass door knobs, wrought iron lamps, and colorful windowboxes of the Back Bays' Romanesque, Queen Anne, and "Chateauesque" rowhouses—whose restrained elegance then stood in stark contrast with the garish residences of New York's first families.

While Victorian Boston didn't covet New York's brash lifestyle, it did admire Gotham's green space; and it asked the designer of Central Park, Frederick Law Olmsted, to landscape the Hub. In 1883 Olmsted moved to the two-acre Fairsted estate in the Boston suburb of Brookline, and over several years laid out his famous but unostentatious "Emerald Necklace" park system. "Boston is the one place in America where wealth and the knowledge of how to use it are apt to coincide,"wrote E.L. Godkin in 1871. Relative to other cities, Boston's opulence has always been understated, if not verging on "reverse snobbery."

In the second half of the 19th century, Boston tripled her physical size with landfill, and soon began to annex neighboring townships like Roxbury, Brighton, South Boston, Dorchester, and Jamaica Plain. Soon after horsedrawn Boston discovered the electric trolley the city's uncorseted growth spilled over into these "streetcar suburbs."

VI

THE VITALITY and expansion of Victorian Boston were more than physical. Minds were being cultivated. Literary circles were feeling their oats. The city was bullish on books.

On arriving in Victorian Boston, Arnold Bennett wrote: "When I got to the entirely admirable hotel, I found a book in a prominent situation on the writing-table in my room. In many hotels this book would have been the Bible. But here was the catalogue of the hotel library; it ran to a hundred and eight-two pages. On the other hand, there was no bar in the hotel and no smoking room."

Boston, with its publishing houses and literary salons, had become a national outlet for the exchange of ideas. It was a port of call for literati from England and the U.S., and it soon won the title, "Athens of America." In Victorian Boston, Henry Adams got his "education" and Ralph Waldo

Emerson argued with Walt Whitman over taking the sex out of *Leaves of Grass*: "...Each point of Emerson's statement was unanswerable, no judge's charge ever more complete or convincing. I could never hear the points better put— and then I felt down in my soul the clear unmistakable conviction to disobey all, and pursue my own way," recalled Whitman. (Without permission, he later printed Emerson's private praise in the front of the second edition: "I greet you at the beginning of a great career.") The crème de la crème of the city's literary culture was the Saturday Club, organized by Emerson himself. Once a month he would interrupt his solitude in Concord for "errands" in Boston and a chance to join such select intellectual companions as Nathaniel Hawthorne, John Greenleaf Whittier, Louis Agassiz and Oliver Wendell Holmes. They dined on seven-course meals and ample servings of lofty conversation.

Later in the 1880s fashionable intellectual discourse continued to move from private residences into the more leisurely setting of exclusive social clubs. On their way home in the evening, if inspired by the "spirit of manumittance," men would stop at the Algonquin or the Union for a fireside chat with chums or a civilized game of billiards. The 20th century's automobile, country club, and urban crime have diminished the quantity of those "clubbing the Hub," but an abundance of venerable institutions remain as rigid as swagger sticks: the Examiner Club, the Somerset, the Union, Algonquin, Tavern, St. Botolph, Chilton, the Club of Odd Volumes, and the Wednesday Evening Club. The Club of Odd Volumes still features on its dinner menu Boston baked beans dished up by the president. The Somerset uses original Daniel Webster silver and Canton china at its meals. (Not long ago the Somerset had a grease fire in its kitchen; and the members reportedly asked the arriving firemen to use the service entrance.)

Ever since Boston's founding days on the Shawmut Peninsula (where Reverend Blackstone assembled his 200-volume book collection in the wilderness), the city has treasured its libraries. James Joyce referred to the Athenaeum —Boston's Rolls Royce in private libraries—as "the place that was to Boston at large as Boston was to the rest of New England." Victorian readers with less fastidious tastes than Joyce, sought out the striking Italian Renaissance public library where they found not only leatherbound classics, but pirate stories, romances, and copies of the city's nine newspapers.

The public library, opened in 1854, was only the first of a variety of educational and cultural institutions which sprouted in the Back Bay during that remarkably fruitful thirty-year period after 1850. Boston College was born in 1863; and, shortly after the Civil War, the Massachusetts Institute of

Technology (MIT) began classes with six professors and eighteen students. In 1867 the New England Conservatory (one of the nation's leading music schools) sounded its opening chords, followed two years later by Boston University—the first American university to admit female applicants on an equal basis with men. The city had become recognized as a great educational center, and Harvard—once that "country college in Cambridge"—was a world renowned institution. It is said, when Bostonian socialites referred to "The President," (even in times of national crisis,) they didn't mean the President of the United States, but the President of Harvard.

In 1881 Major Henry Lee Higginson founded the Boston Symphony Orchestra, complemented four years later by the birth of the less formal "middlebrow" Boston Pops Orchestra—still going strong under the leadership of "Boston's Music Man" Arthur Fiedler. In 1871 the Museum of Fine Arts was established. It now houses, among much other treasure, a superb collection of French Impressionists, and "the most beautiful woman in Boston"— a 2,400-year-old Aphrodite known as the "Bartlett head."

We cannot leave the arts in Boston without tipping our historical hat to the greatest of the Victorian grandes dames: Isabella Stewart Gardner. Daughter of a New York dry-goods merchant, she married Boston in the form of John Lowell Gardner, son of the last of the city's East India merchants. "Mrs. Jack" moved to Beacon Street with her new spouse and proceeded to politely bulldoze her way into Boston's most exclusive social circles. In addition to the legends she left behind (most of them true, no doubt), Mrs. Gardner built a Venetian palace in the Fenway marshes to house her European art treasures. The structure was referred to by commoners as "Mrs. Jack's I-talian palace;" and it remains one of the finest small art museums in the nation.

If Isabella Stewart Gardner did nothing else, she dynamited Boston's staid stereotype of Victorian women and added momentum to the feminist movement which was well under way. In 1868 a core of female intellectuals and reformists had founded the first women's club in Boston, with the help of ardent feminist Julia Ward Howe, author of "The Battle Hymn of the Republic." Boston was also the headquarters for the American Women's Suffrage Association, the country's first city women's club, as well as the home of the Women's Journal, a 19th century precursor of *Ms.* magazine.

Feminism was hardly an isolated instance of Boston's ameliorative zeal. Ever since the first half of the 19th century, the city's pride and idealism had surfaced in a string of reform movements: women's rights, temperance, nativism, and anti-slavery. It was in Boston that abolitionist William Lloyd Garrison ("I will be as harsh as truth and uncompromising as justice") founded his radical anti-slavery magazine, *The Liberator*. Long before the Civil War, prominent Bostonians were supporting the "underground railroad;" and many donated money to John Brown for his hapless assault on Harper's Ferry. Victorian Boston, the "city of conscience," gained a reputation for its championing individual rights. It was said to have more reform organizations per square acre than any other American city.

By the end of the 19th century, however, Boston's self-improving spirit began to wane as dramatically as it had waxed. The high noon of confidence merged into a long afternoon of complacency. The fashionable were collecting grandfather clocks, pewter plates, and tall tales of the glorious past. In the midst of Boston's uncertain present and less certain future, the city grew nostalgic. Van Wyck Brooks wrote, "Over-intelligent, fragile, cautious, and doubtful, the soul of the culture-city loses the self-confidence and joy that have marked its early development. What has once been vital becomes provincial; and the sense that one belongs to a dying race dominates and poisons the creative mind."

Mr. Brooks' obituary was a trifle premature.

VII

AT THE turn of the century, the city was under attack—intellectually and economically. Some of Harvard's new graduates, such as John Reed and Walter Lippmann, were living in New York's Greenwich Village and verbally assaulting Boston's Victorian strait-laced morality and ivory tower conservatism. Upton Sinclair came from California to protest the city's legal ban on his book *Oil*, which was in part an exposé of the Harding Administration. New York continued to drain off Boston's shipping, and the once wealthy port was going broke. In the 1920's textile mills and shoe factories began packing up their looms and stitchers, and heading south to cheaper labor and lower taxes.

While Manhattan and Chicago bristled with skyscraper monuments to their commercial prominence in the first half of the century, Boston's urban landscape lay dormant. Between 1929 and 1959, only two major buildings were erected downtown.

Despite the town's reputation for unswerving historic preservation, what restrained the wrecker's ball was not so much Boston's sense of history, as her inability to pay a wrecker. Her success in saving face (architectural face, at least) has been the result more of early accident than of recent intent.

Since 1960, Boston has refused to sit still long enough to have its portrait painted—an impatience which continues to upset the city's more adamant preservationists. They knit their brows over the "Manhattanization" of the cityscape with the new skyscraper spine of downtown bank buildings, the fifty-two-story Prudential Tower, and that mirrored monolith, the John Hancock Tower. Urban architecture fanatics wonder if perhaps Frank Lloyd Wright was correct when he suggested of Boston that someone should "clear out the eight hundred thousand people and preserve it as a museum." More practical-minded preservationists, however, saw that, after filling its bays and annexing nearby towns, Boston had no choice but to grow *up*.

Today Boston is a tall tale of two cities: antique and modern living side by side. Prison cells (of the eighty-eight-old Boylston Street police station) has become galleries for the Institute of Contemporary Art. The Warren Tavern in Charlestown—said to have been a haunt of Paul Revere—was recently restored, and caters at lunchtime to a sophisticated City Hall crowd.

As enamored of the historic as Boston is, the city is unlikely to become another Williamsburg; Yankee practicality and ingenuity would not permit it. "You can't pickle a city," says Walter Muir Whitehill who owns an 18th century chair "because I want to sit on it."

Boston's mid-century renaissance was apparent not only in the architecture, but in the city's economy. The technological revolution of the 1950s placed a high value on the brainpower of Boston's universities. In 1960 a Boston boy was elected President of the United States, and promised to put a man on the moon by the end of the decade. More than 350 aerospace, engineering, electronics and technological firms—together with various and sundry "think tanks"—blossomed along Boston's circumferential highway Route 128, soon dubbed the "Space Highway" and "Research Row."

The city also benefited from the breath of fresh air imported with a new breed of youth seeking their fortunes in Boston, despite warnings that the cost of living was the highest in the continental U.S. Ivy Leaue graduates were polled as to the American city in which they would most like to live and work; they put Boston at the top. (No doubt one reason for the city's popularity with the nation's youth was the Hub's tendency to surround herself with exquisite neighbors—the beaches of Cape Cod, the ski trails of New Hampshire's White Mountains, the rocky Maine coast.)

Boston is young and single. Two-fifths of its residents are under twenty-five years old, and three-fifths of the population is unmarried—both statistics largely attributable to the high concentration of colleges. Detroit has its autoworkers, St. Petersburg its retirees, but Boston is known for its students; more than 200,000 of them attend some 65 degree-granting institutions of higher learning. Boston is the ultimate center of scholarship—or the ultimate playpen for college kids depending on whom you ask.

At the peak of Boston's academic pyramid (which includes Wellesley, Tufts, Brandeis, Boston College, Boston University, Simmons and Northeastern) are two superpowers on the Cambridge side of the Charles River: Harvard-Radcliffe and the Massachusetts Institute of Technology (MIT). In the (usually peaceful) world of Harvard Yard, undergraduates laze beneath leafy oaks, perusing a volume of Proust, or Samuelson's introductory economics text or the latest *New York Review of Books*. In this haven of quiet, one can almost hear the ivy climbing deliberately up the red-brick dormitory walls. However, step into Harvard Square (the site on which the village of Cambridge was founded and named after the English university town), and you are in another world: a twenty-four-hour proper playground of bookstores, coffeehouses, tobacco shops and tweedy clothing stores catering to a J. Pressed clientele; a potpourri of street musicians playing Bartók and bluegrass; vendors peddling pottery and pot; hawkers waving broadsides advertising a one-man puppet show or a lecture by B.F. Skinner.

A fifteen-minute hitchhike down "Mass. Ave." toward Boston, stands Harvard's Cambridge neighbor, MIT, (frequently called "Tech"). MIT is most famous for its discovery of radar, and synthetic penicillin, its development of digital computers, its science advisors to the White House, and its Nobel prize-winning professors. Behind the astrophysics, logarithms, and pocket calculators (packed on hips like six-shooters), however, lurks an inventive sense of humor. In years past, MIT has given the city a tiddlywinks marathon, an international Frisbee championship, the world's longest yo-yo, and Boston's only unicycling club.

Beside the scholars at Harvard, MIT, and three score other colleges, Boston has "enrolled" another army of students who attend no academic institutions, and leave the city with no sheepskins. They come to learn from "wise old Boston," and are willing to take jobs as waitresses and taxi drivers. They spend free time in bookstores or at discotheques in Kenmore Square, watching Bergman at the Orson Wells Cinema, or munching a mung bean sandwich at the Golden Temple Conscious Cookery.

There seems to be room for anyone in this beguiling city which has no qualms about flouting tradition with the propriety of eccentricity, finding its future in its past, being suitably stuffy, yet friendly enough to boil a cup of broth for a sick neighbor, and open-minded enough to tolerate anything under the sun—including petty provincialism.

Boston is Everyman's university.

VII

BEYOND BRICKS AND BRAHMINS

THERE ARE centuries and hordes of Boston's sons and lovers, and I shamelessly fall into the latter category. Neither born nor bred (nor even schooled) here, I am Bostonian by choice and conviction. I've lived in its ethnic enclaves, snooped through its architecture and alleys, and have come to at least one conclusion: There's more to Boston than Paul Revere, "Old Ironsides," and Bunker Hill. There's more to this city than the symphony orchestra, a seafood dinner, and the next plane to New York. There's more to Boston's spectrum than red bricks, brownstones, and bluenoses.

The city's heart beats strongest in the neighborhoods—its principal source of character and clannishness. Ask any Bostonian what is his hometown, and the reply will not be "Boston." He is more likely to respond the "North End," "East Boston," "Southie," "Brighton," "West Roxbury," and so on. The city is a patchwork of some twenty distinct ethnic urban villages, many with their own cuisine, fashions, accent (or language), and frequently their own "Little City Hall." These cocoons of tradition are so varied and vital that they defy the impersonal sameness of metropolitan concrete and bureaucracy. "We're big enough to be a city, but small enough to handle our problems. If we can't do it here, it's over for America," says Roxbury's Elma Lewis, once described as "Black America's Sol Hurok, Tyrone Guthrie and P.T. Barnum combined."

Nobody can comprehend and appreciate the city in one visit or one lifetime. There are always new faces to discover, new friends to make. So permit me to introduce a few of my favorite people from the neighborhoods. They tell me they are the only ones who understand this crazy quilt of a city. I tend to believe them.

If the wind is right when you fly into Logan Airport, you'll pass a few hundred feet over a tiny double-decker house in East Boston, not far from the runway. That's Anna's house—Anna DeFronzo, "everybody's grandmother." Like the blue-haired ladies on Beacon Hill, Anna is a proud preservationist.

A few years ago she climbed onto a bulldozer to prevent the destruction of an historic park near her home. This was not her only feat of constructive obstruction. There was the time when she and the "Maverick Street mothers," armed with baby carriages, halted trucks carrying landfill for the airport expansion that was nibbling at their backyards. Her reputation has grown so that now astute politicians, from City Hall to Congress, always "check first with Anna."

Anna is not the only East Bostonian with a reputation. There's Tony, an Italian chef who makes the best dish of scampi in the city, and is notorious for adorning his restaurant walls with souvenirs confiscated from customers—neckties and scraps of clothing.

A tortellini's throw across Boston Harbor—or a 25¢ ride through the Sumner Tunnel—lies the North End, an Italian neighborhood where you'll find another master of "Old Country" cuisine: Joseph Memmolo cranks carpets of yellow egg noodles out of a clanky tomato-red assemblyline, and daily slices them into ribbons and strings for his customers.

Further south along the waterfront is South Boston, a white working-class neighborhood of longshoremen, cops, firemen and truckers. There you'll also find five miles of the city's best beach, as well as an abundance of proud Irish. Southie's Irish are today outnumbered two-to-one by Italians, Poles and Lithuanians, but the neighborhood's flavor remains decidedly Celtic. Families are knit as tight as tweed caps, and if your Irish neighbors aren't blood relatives, their ancestral friendship probably dates back to pre-Potato Famine days in Waterford or Galway counties, Ireland. In Southie, it is said, you can hardly walk a block down Broadway Street without running into an uncle or niece, or a buddy from the candlepin league, VFW post, Knights of Columbus, or the housing project where you grew up.

Next door to Southie's famous L Street Bath House, a sixty-nine-year old tap dancer-comedienne-bandleader, named Nellie Gorham, strikes up her Senior Serenaders for a chorus of "Sweet Rosie O'Grady" or "Mother Machree" every St. Patrick's Day. Nellie, decked out in her green polka-dot dress and armed with her trusty ukulele or single-stringed washtub bass, is backed up by a beehive of kazoo and washboard musicians. They perform with the enthusiasm of a team of high school cheerleaders, and are all over sixty-five-years old.

Cross the South Boston Bridge to the South End, once fashionable, now largely dilapidated. From the Syrian grocery store on Shawmut Avenue and Puerto Rican housing project on Pembroke Street, to the Chinese Laundry on Tremont and the Black storefront music school on Columbus, the South End specializes in variety, if not ethnic eccentricity. Harry Kamenides, otherwise known as "Harry the Greek," thrives here. He runs a bargain-hunter's paradise amid the South End's boarded up storefronts and sidewalk trash; and he sells everything from spats and green peppers, to roller skates and monogrammed overalls. He once sold Cliff Robertson a pair of shoes, and still supplies Harvard and MIT students with top hats and tails.

"Positively no changing of socks in this store," is a sign at the cash register; and: "We have coats to fit billy goats." While shopping you'll no doubt hear the fuzzy Greek music drifting from the transistor radio near the door; and you may even catch a glimpse of Harry dancing, barechested, snapping his fingers over his head, and singing the lyrics to the store's pep song (which he composed): "Oooga-mooga-uga-jooga-tooga-bambalooga." Most of the other Greeks in the neighborhood have left the decaying Dover Street neighborhood and headed for the suburbs. Why does Harry stick around? His son Milton grins: "Have you ever tried to move a landmark?"

Harry's establishment may not suit the aesthetic sophistication of some culture vultures. For them, right up the street, is the new Boston Center for the Arts, which hosts everything from flea markets to one of the finest ballet companies in the country. Just north of the BCA is Boston's own "Forbidden City" in a twelve-block area, Chinatown. Here East meets West. Telephone booths have pagoda tops; a Taoist yin-yang is painted on the basketball court at the YMCA; portraits of Sun Yat-Sen and George Washington stand shoulder to shoulder in public places.

In a tropical basement on Chinatown's Tyler Street, Lee Chun spends $10,000 each year watering a rain forest of bean sprouts. His subterranean laboratory is covered with a maze of plastic trash buckets, funnels, magnifying glasses, tubing and counterweights—ingeniously strung together with electrical tape. It's all part of his business of turning fifteen pounds of Oklahoma mung beans into ninety pounds of sprouts.

If leaving Chinatown via Stuart Street, stop by Jacob Wirth's, a German eating establishment dating from 1917. It has retained its dark wooden floors, pinwheel fans, and stout waiters with thick Bismarkian brogues; and it serves Teutonic splendors: bulky portions of boiled potatoes, red cabbage, bratwurst, and smoked ham. "Jake" Wirth's is in the center of Boston's theater district, and waiters specialize in getting customers to the 8 o'clock shows.

A walk up Washington Street, through the Combat Zone's x-rated arcade of exotica and erotica, leads you to Boylston Street and the Boston Common. From there the glorious glint of the State House dome beckons one to downtown's social and topographical summit—Beacon Hill. But who lives on the "other side of the Hill," beyond Acorn Street, Louisburg Square, the quaint cobblestones, and the elegant townhouses? Joel Cohen, for one, in a ramshackle, walk-up, Garden Street apartment. Amid a chaotic clutter of Breughel prints, record albums and dinner dishes, this leading lutist is engineering the revival of medieval music. He conducts (left-handed) the

Boston Camerata; and he straddles centuries and continents. Joel may appear to spend most of his waking hours in the Middle Ages, but he relishes reading Boston's very modern underground press.

Amid the collage of characters on nearby Newbury Street is Brother Blue, a professional storyteller with a Ph.D. who performs in Emmanuel Church. In a cloud of bells, balloons, and butterflies, Dr. Hugh Morgan Hill, this inner-city bard travels from prisons to faculty clubs, spinning tales which bring laughter ("Little Blue Riding Hood") and heal racial strife ("The Rainbow Child").

He sings and dances into the hearts of scholars and street people. He discovers the extraordinary in the commonplace. He finds rainbows in children's smiles. "My only quest," says Brother Blue," is to bring out the beautiful butterfly, the ever-perfect story, that hides in the cocoon we call me and you."

A few more blocks up Newbury Street, works another artist—a painter who uses Boston as his canvas. People sit daily on Robert Rossi's art work, which is shown everywhere from the governor's suite to the Boston Garden. Carl Yastrzemski blasts doubles off it. Bostonians are surrounded by it. In the basement of Johnson's Paint Company, Bob is employed as the city's last full-time paint mixer.

His spruce green covers the left field wall in Fenway Park, and his yellow makes a line around the Bruins hockey rink. Forested with aisles of drooling paint cans, his spattered floors rival Jackson Pollock's best.

Perhaps this parade of characters confirms Boston's eccentricity—perhaps its humanity, perhaps its diversity. Boston is a city of contradictions where the crazy and the quiet live side by side and may not always mix, nor would they care to mix. The Emersonian notion of Boston's melting pot never did materialize. The only pot Boston resembles today is a pot of rich ethnic stew filled with chili peppers, matzo balls, collard greens, water chestnuts—you name it. Such diverse ingredients don't always go well together in the same bite; nevertheless their juxtaposition keeps the diet interesting. Planted in uniformity, Boston flowered in variety. The cold marble of Puritan rectitude has made way for humanity's frailty, grace and warmth.

No doubt the city's universities, banks, museums, bricks and mortar will continue to represent the town's history; but somehow the neighborhoods will always be the city's future. Bostonians, proper and otherwise, will continue to march in her parades, pilot her tugs, make her music, cheer her athletes, grow her bean sprouts, parent her children, complain and brag about her prospects. These characters may not always make the headlines. They will always make Boston.

OLD STATE HOUSE: LONE SURVIVOR IN A SKYSCRAPER CANYON

Probably nothing has heaped greater glory on the Old State House than its extraordinary capacity to survive and hold a predatory city at bay. It was erected in 1713 to replace Boston's first town house, a wooden structure consumed by flames two years earlier; and its stout brick walls successfully resisted a devastating fire in 1747 that gutted the rest of the building. By 1750 it had been rebuilt and, according to a diarist, "embellished with a great cupola...which on rejoycing days is elluminated."

It was here in the Council Chamber, in 1761, that patriot firebrand James Otis fulminated against British "writs of assistance," which he considered illegal. Years later John Adams, who had watched spellbound as Otis thundered his defiance of "this monster of oppression," wrote: "Then and there the child Independence was born."

It was a snowy March 5, 1770, when the long-simmering dispute between Massachusetts and the Mother Country claimed its first victims in the Boston Massacre. The trouble began beneath the eastern balcony of the Old State House. Whether by design or chance, a mob gathered around an unfortunate British private, and began pelting him with snowballs, sticks, and pieces of ice. A squad from his regiment doubled to his rescue, and when one of the redcoats was felled with a cudgel he opened fire. The others followed suit. Three of the mob slumped dead in the snow. Another two lay dying.

A considerably more amiable crowd gathered beneath the Old State House six years later to hear the Declaration of Independence read from the balcony, and to watch as the lion and unicorn surmounting the building were torn down and burned. No longer symbols of a distant tyranny, a new pair of royal beasts have since been mounted on their perches atop the russet brickwork.

Thereafter the Old State House fell into decline, and in 1830 emerged as Boston City Hall. It again caught fire; and in 1844 it was leased for commercial purposes. Today the Old State House stands as an island of colonial charm amidst the anonymous products of 20th century architecture—an historic building celebrated as much for its resilience as for the momentous events within and outside its walls.

The Freedom Trail, that red striped historic honor roll, snakes beneath the Old State House balcony, and past a triangular traffic island punctuated with a circle of stonework said to mark the site of the Boston Massacre.

CITY HALL: AZTEC TEMPLE IN A "BRICK DESERT"?

At least one critic has called the new City Hall Plaza "Boston's brick desert." But a very different opinion is held by Walter Muir Whitehill, the venerable Boston historian and twenty-six-year director of the Athenaeum (a private library): "The City Hall is low and huge, with Mycenean or Aztec overtones in its massiveness. In my view it is as fine a building for its time and place as Boston has ever produced," he writes in *Boston, A Topographical History*. Whitehill had good reason to be pleased. He collaborated with the architect, renowned I.M. Pei, in Government Center's master plan. Under this plan the brick plaza integrates "New Boston" with such surrounding historic sites as the Old State House, Sears Crescent, Faneuil Hall, Quincy Market and the North End.

Standing at the heart of Government Center, City Hall is built on the site of notorious Scollay Square, a garish honky-tonk district where generations of sailors amused themselves in bars, burlesque theaters, shooting galleries and tattoo studios, while their warships underwent repairs in the Boston Navy Yard.

The design of the City Hall itself was determined through a national competition which attracted 250 entries. From these Boston selected the young, relatively unknown New York architectural firm of Kallmann, McKinnell and Knowles. Boston's official Bicentennial Guide book offers this explanation: "Both the structure and its surrounding funneling plaza represent the ideals of openness and accessibility in city government."

STATE HOUSE AND COMMON: FEEDING GROUNDS FOR LAWMAKERS AND COLONIAL COWS

The gold dome on Charles Bulfinch's State House has not always glinted in the sunlight. Before the ubiquitous Paul Revere sheathed it in copper in 1802, it was painted a dull gray. It was gilded in 1861, but the dome was not covered with gold leaf until 1874. During the Second World War it was blackened for fear Nazi submarines would use it as a navigational aid.

Boston's venerable Common, spread out in front of the State House, gives the city a bucolic air. "From the earliest times until after Boston became a city, the tinkling of bells and lowing of cattle might be heard across its hills and dales," notes an historian. The first settlers had bought some forty-eight acres from hermit Rev. William Blackstone in 1634, and set it apart for "common use"—for the "feeding of cattel" and as a "place for a trayning field." A law of 1640 states that "there shall be no land granted out of ye open ground or Common field." Today no part of the Common—the oldest public park in America—can be sold or built on without the consent of the citizens of Boston. Writer Robert Shackleton asserted during World War I, "The people of Boston will retain their liberty so long as they retain their Common, and will sink into commonplaceness only if they give up their Common. It is, in a double sense a common heritage."

36

WATERFRONT NEIGHBORS: A "NEW" WAREHOUSE AND AN "OLD" SKYSCRAPER

The gilt sign of the Chart House Restaurant partly frames the U.S. Custom House tower—Boston's oldest skyscraper. The swank restaurant is housed in the Gardiner Building, a rare surviving 18th century warehouse, renovated in 1973. It retains the original wood beams, floors, staircase and red brick walls and rests on Long Wharf, the most famous wharfage in colonial Boston.

Built in 1710 by Captain Oliver Noyes, Long Wharf was lined with brick warehouses, auction halls, shops and counting houses on its north side, and it eventually ran some 2,000 feet out into the harbor. British troops landed here in 1768, at the tip of the wharf. They came ashore with a train of artillery and, according to Paul Revere, "there formed and marched with insolent parade, drums beatting, fifes playing." It was from Long Wharf that men of the 5th and 38th Regiments of Foot set off for the Battle of Bunker Hill. On March 17, 1776, fleeing from General Washington's cannons set on Dorchester Heights, the entire British garrison marched down onto this wharf and evacuated Boston for Halifax—never to return.

Until the mid-19th century, Boston Harbor was jammed with clipper ships bound for exotic ports, and Atlantic Avenue bustled with saloons of sailors and warehouses stuffed with produce. But New York soon took over as the East Coast's chief commercial port, and the Boston waterfront fell into decay for a century.

Not until the city's architectural renaissance in the late 1960s and early 1970s, were the abandoned granite and brick warehouses on Lewis and Commercial Wharves resurrected—and not as warehouses, but as classy apartments, restaurants and boutiques. Wood-carved, gold letter signs now advertise the new wares of the waterfront: architectural consulting, plant shops, Scandianavian design furniture.

38

A RARE SAIL AT LONG WHARF

Long Wharf was once a forest of masts and furled canvas. Sailing ships from all over the world put into Boston with every imaginable commodity in their holds. Beating into the port in 1836, Richard Henry Dana noted that "vessels began to multiply until the bay seemed actually alive with sails gliding about in every direction; some on the wind, and others before it, as they were bound to or from the emporium of trade and centre of the bay." In the 18th century, Boston merchants grew rich, shipping salt cod to the West Indies, sailing on to England with fish, sugar, tobacco, and molasses, and bearing home a whole variety of British products needed in the growing Massachusetts Bay Colony. Later, when Boston built distilleries, a rum trade developed with West Africa, in exchange for slaves, ivory, gold dust, and mahogany. The slaves were carried to the West Indies where they were exchanged for the molasses that fed the ravenous rum industry.

In 1748—a year when 430 vessels tied up at Boston's wharves and 540 cast off from them—a member of the colony's House of Representatives suggested "leave might be given to hang up a representation of a Cod Fish in the room where the House sits, as a memorial of the importance of the Cod Fishery to the welfare of the nation." A large wooden cod was duly installed, and the humble fish, or at least a successor, hangs in the State House today.

Besides recalling the foundations of the city's prosperity, the sight of sails at Long Wharf stirs memories of the sleek clipper ships built by Donald McKay in his East Boston yards. *The Flying Cloud* was the most famous of his graceful creations. On her maiden voyage in 1851, she sped from New York to San Francisco via Cape Horn in eighty-nine days. In 1852 he built *Sovereign of the Seas*; and the following year his masterpiece, *Great Republic* was christened. A granite obelisk at Boston's Castle Island commemorates this "Master-Builder, whose genius produced ships of beauty and speed before unknown which swept the Seven Seas, made the American Clipper Ship famous the world over, and brought renown and prosperity to the City of Boston."

OLD CORNER BOOKSTORE: LITERARY PORT OF CALL

During the 19th century, the Old Corner Bookstore was the nation's literary port of call for noted English and American authors such as Emerson, Hawthorne, Dickens, Thackeray, Julia Ward Howe and Harriet Beecher Stowe. The crowd was select, and in some cases so were their reading habits. Oliver Wendell Holmes, a regular at the Old Corner Bookstore expressed his concern that "One who has had the mischance to soil his mind reading certain poems of Swift will never cleanse it to its original wholeness."

The colonial brick dwelling, built in 1711 for an apothecary, was converted into a bookstore in 1828. Five years later it was purchased and made famous by William Ticknor and James Fields, the first genius of American publishing. Fields, with his wife Annie, later gathered gifted literati to their salon in what Henry James called the "Charles Street Waterside Museum." The host was a noted author and conversationalist; and he set aside a ground floor office in the Old Corner Bookstore, from which he launched *The Atlantic Monthly* in 1857. It was then the voice of liberal, enlightened Boston, and is still the oldest general magazine published in the United States. The store soon became a bustling clubhouse of those literary giants who earned Boston its title—the "Athens of America."

The glitter of Boston's Gilded Age faded in the late 19th century. The literary salons and clubs became more comfortable but less productive as laboratories for fresh thought. The high achievements and rigors of the past were replaced with dreams of nostalgia. In spite of the gasping vigor of the Gay 90s, Boston turned to preserving leather-bound volumes of Longfellow rather than nurturing young authors. In 1880, William Dean Howells left the city for New York, calling Boston a "death-in-life" town. Ambition had atrophied, said Henry Adams, who departed for Washington, D.C. because "Boston seemed to offer no market for educated labor." Henry James moved to England.

With the book-writers went the bookstores; the last bookseller departed the Old Corner Bookstore in 1903, and the building fell upon hard times. In 1960 it narrowly escaped demolition. Today, tastefully restored, it houses the classified advertising and subscription offices of *The Boston Globe*.

ISABELLA STEWART GARDNER MUSEUM: MRS. JACK'S TREASURE HOUSE

Isabella Stewart Gardner was Boston society's greatest grande dame. A brilliant, charming, and curvaceous millionairess, she alternately dazzled and shocked a strait-laced city. Her indulgence was shameless; "C'est mon plaisir" was her motto. Unabashedly eccentric, she quaffed beer, toyed with Buddhism, told risque stories; and when guests attended her "at-homes" in her Beacon Street house, she was quite capable of greeting them from a perch in the lower branches of a mimosa tree. At Lent she was given to scrubbing the steps of a local church to atone for her sins. But her real weakness was art. She collected it fanatically.

With her husband, wealthy Yankee John Lowell Gardner, whom she married in 1860, she amassed a vast array of art treasures on trips to Europe and Asia, buying her first important picture—a Madonna by Francisco Zurbarán—in Seville in 1888. While attending art history lectures at Harvard she met the gifted young Bernard Berenson, and when he graduated in 1887 she paid for him to study in Europe. Subsequently he became her chief advisor in the acquisition of art works.

In 1891 she inherited $2,750,000 from her father; and when her husband died seven years later, leaving her a further $3,000,000, she decided it was time to house the priceless collection they had acquired. (Including such masterpieces as Titian's "Rape of Europa," Rembrandt's "Storm of the Sea of Galilee," and Vermeer's "The Concert," her "treasure house" remains one of the finest small museums in the nation, and today offers free classical in the Tapestry Room three times a week.)

"Mrs. Jack"—as Boston affectionately called her—acted with characteristic panache. She decided to ship an entire Venetian palazzo, stone by stone, to the marshes of Boston's Fenway in the Back Bay. She personally supervised the construction of the building, ordering workmen around with a trumpet, until it was finished. When the palace opened to the public in 1903, it was as if the Venetian Renaissance had been reincarnated in 20th century Boston. The scent of flowers wafted up from the court into galleries splendid with paintings, drawings, sculpture, furniture, tapestries, glass, and ceramics. Mrs. Gardner died in 1924, bequeathing her treasures to the public on the condition that nothing be moved on penalty of the museum and its contents being sold and the money donated to Harvard University. And so her pleasure is still her pleasure after all.

44

THE COBBLED CHARM OF ACORN STREET

Acorn Street enjoys the distinction of being the narrowest of Beacon Hill's narrow streets, and one of the few to retain an expanse of time-smoothed cobbles. In the heyday of the horse and carriage, many a coachman employed by the Hill's great houses lived here. It is a little world of lavender window panes, bootscrapers, gaslights, old carriage houses, hidden gardens, and wrought iron balconies.

Originally named for the crude tar-burning "lighthouse" on its crest, Beacon Hill had sixty feet shaved off its original height at a time when landfill was more valuable than vistas. But this did not lower its social elevation, which increased steadily during the 19th century so that Robert Shackleton could write in 1917: "Beacon Hill, the height of exclusiveness, the citadel of aristocracy, all this it has long been, as if its being a hill aided in giving it literal unapproachableness. It still retains its prideful poise in outward and visible signs of its perfectly cared-for houses and correctness of dress and manners and equipage."

The 1870s witnessed a mass migration of Beacon Hill's Brahmins to fashionable addresses in "the inscrutable, the unknowable back Bay." Around the turn of the century, however, the old houses on "the Hill" were "rediscovered," and the values of homes soared. In Louisburg Square, for example, prices rose from $14,800 in 1910 to a whopping $140,000 price tag today. Beacon Hill's heritage became so valued that in the 1950s the residents staged a "sit-out" in their rocking chairs to save their warm red brick sidewalks. In 1963 the Hill was designated a Registered National Historic Landmark.

46

THE GLASS MENAGERIE

Few modern buildings have suffered such agonizing birth pangs as Boston's tallest skyscraper, the sixty-story John Hancock Tower, It is seen here dwarfing the New England Mutual Life Insurance Building, and reflecting a spectral image on the old Hancock headquarters.

At the beginning of its construction, foundation excavation jostled the Back Bay's soggy landfill, subsequently damaging water and sewer mains, and shifting surrounding streets and sidewalks. Soon after the tower had been completed, it started to mysteriously shed its glass skin: some 3,500 of the structure's 10,344 mirrored Thermopanes had to be replaced with plywood sheets to prevent further cracking and popping. The mirrored giant, designed by I.M. Pei and Partners, was dubbed the "plywood palace," and overnight became the neighborhood joke of the Back Bay. Finally all 13.5 acres of the glass in the luckless building had to be replaced with a specially tempered variety at an additional cost of $7.7 million. Still more "extras" were needed: Hancock officials ordered a $3 million, 600-ton "shock absorber" system of weights to damp down the building's wind sway.

When panes of the new glass unaccountably began shattering in early 1976, Boston's building commissioner suspended the tower's occupancy permit until that summer. Prestigious tenants cancelled leases, and parishioners of the adjoining Trinity Church sued for $4 million, alleging that construction had caused their edifice to tilt. Legal suits flew thick and fast. In April, 1976, five years and $52 million past the original occupancy target (the total cost had reached $144 million), only six floors of the glass skyscraper had been occupied. Perhaps the ultimate architectural irony of New England's highest building (forty feet higher than its competitor's Prudential Tower) is that it was constructed on the site of old Westminster Hotel, which years ago was forced to remove its upper story because it violated the stringent height regulations of Copley Square.

48

BOSTON PUBLIC LIBRARY: "THE PEOPLE'S PALACE"

Boston is bullish on books. It always has been. Nearly half of Boston's residents are registered to borrow volumes from public libraries, and it is not unusual at peaks in the academic year to see scores and scores of students waiting for the doors of the Boston Public Library to open on a Sunday afternoon. At such times an average of 1,000 people go through the library turnstiles every hour.

During the academic year, the city bursts its seams with nearly 200,000 students. Their arrival on Labor Day is signalled by the caravan of U-Haul trailers on Beacon Street. Their departure in June is attested the day commuters can again find a seat in the subway. Come Christmas time, the city exhales as the academic army leaves for skiing in Aspen or sunning in Fort Lauderdale; some, inevitably, are left behind to man the academic fort. Boston possesses sixty-five institutions of higher learning, and most of them close their libraries during the Yuletide holiday, to save on fuel and utility costs. So the Boston Public Library has become the Christmas stronghold for students cramming for January exams and adding the final footnotes to their term papers.

Founded in 1852, the BPL is the oldest, free, tax-supported municipal library in the world. Among its American peers, it ranks second in size only to the New York Public Library.

The BPL's eastern facade is shown here, mottled by light from a passing cloud reflected off the mirror-sheathed Hancock Tower across the street. The library stands as both an architectural monument and a testament to Boston's love of learning. In designing this "Great Palace of Books," architect Charles Follen McKim drew inspiration from Henri Labrouste's Bibliotheque Ste-Genevieve in Paris. The Renaissance-style building, built in 1895 around a charming central courtyard is known for its noble stairway of orange Sienna marble, Edwin Abbey's mural paintings depicting the "Quest of the Holy Grail," and a majestic barrel-vaulted reading room which would give Oxford's Bodleian a run for its manuscripts. Further embellishment is added by the John Singer Sargent's sandstone gallery decorations, and the Puvis de Chavannes murals over the staircase—judged by Arnold Bennett to be "unsurpassed works of art, which alone would suffice to make Boston a place of pilgrimage."

50

OLD NORTH STEEPLE: "ONE, IF BY LAND, AND TWO, IF BY SEA"

When watchers in Charlestown saw two lanterns flickering from this steeple on April 18, 1775, they knew the redcoats were sallying out "by sea." Paul Revere had arranged for the young sexton Robert Newman to flash the signal before the silversmith rowed across the harbor to begin his momentous ride.

Old North Church (or more accurately, Christ Church) was built in 1723; but it did not get its 191-foot steeple until 1740, when a group of Honduras merchants put up the money for it. The tallest in Boston, it served as a useful landmark for ships approaching the harbor. When a hurricane wrecked the steeple in 1804, a new one was erected from a design by Charles Bulfinch, distinguished architect of early Federal Boston. That in turn was blown over by a hurricane in 1954, and replaced with a copy of the original colonial structure.

Incredible as it may seem, one John Childs appears to have actually flown from the Old North steeple on September 13, 1757—though by what means remains unknown. The day after, flushed with success, he repeated the performance, not once but twice, for awed crowds. On the second flight, if an account can be believed, "he set off with two pistols loaded, one of which he discharged in his descent, the other missing fire, he cocked and snap't it again before he reached the place prepared to receive him." His daredevilry, however, offended the stern work ethic of Boston's citizens; for it is recorded that, as his "performance lead many people from their business, he is forbid flying any more in the town."

Old North is as famous for the grave beauty of its steeple as it is for the "royal peal" of its eight bells, considered the best and sweetest in America. The largest weighs 1,545 pounds and the smallest 620 pounds. One is inscribed: "We are the first ring of bells cast for the British Empire in North America. A.R. Ano 1744." The "A.R." stands for master bell-maker Abel Rudhall of Gloucester, England.

COPP'S HILL BURYING GROUND: "HERE LIES..."

Bostonians are not known to boast; but they are too proud to bury their history. And when they do bury those who made history, they somehow never forget them.

The founding Puritans were obsessed with the subject of death, and gravestones were big business; so much so that the average rich merchant gave more business to colonial artisans at the time of his passing than during his life. Consequently, downtown Boston still has three famous burial grounds, which provide a great source of history and green space.

The site of a windmill in 1632, Copp's Hill (named after the original owner of the land, William Copp) became a burial ground in 1659 or 1660. British cannons placed in this cemetery during the battle of Bunker Hill in 1775, helped burn Charlestown to the ground with a bombardment of pitch-filled shot. Judging from the bullet marks in some of the slate headstones, the British also tried some target practice.

The Reverend Doctors (Cotton, Samuel and Increase) Mather lie here. Cotton, fervid pastor and relentless pursuer of witches, must surely have uttered the most damning stricture ever passed on Boston when he declared it "almost a Hell upon earth, a city full of Lies and Murders and Blasphemies; a dismal Picture and an Emblem of Hell." Sharing the cemetery with the Mathers are Edmund Hartt, builder of the USS *Constitution*, and Robert Newman who hung the famous lanterns in nearby Old North Church for Paul Revere.

One gravestone describes its occupant as "An eminent merchant, an honorable counselor, and a despiser of sorry persons and little actions." Elsewhere in the cemetery, a uxorious sexton has marked the grave of his wife: "Betsy, wife of David Darling, died Mar. 23, 1805. She was the mother of 17 children and around her lies 12 of them and two were lost at sea. Brother sextons: Please leave a clear berth for me near this stone."

Many of the names in this North End graveyard are strangely moving: Love Rawlins, Mehitable Scarlett, Silence Barnard, Temperance Coleman. For every distinguished occupant there are scores of ordinary citizens here whose sweat and sinew helped build Boston.

KING'S CHAPEL BURYING GROUND: WHERE PURITANS SLEEP

The notorious Captain Kidd, whose privateering in Massachusetts waters smacked so much of piracy that he was put to death for it, supposedly lies in this sleepy graveyard. In fact, he is far more likely buried in Wapping, England, as he was hanged there at Execution Dock in 1701. There is no doubt, however, that John Winthrop slumbers here. That "famous Pattern of Piety and Justice" founded Boston in 1630 with his gritty band of Puritans.

The graveyard, which nestles against the granite mass of King's Chapel, was originally Puritan Isaac Johnson's vegetable garden. But when the venerable Brother, in accordance with his wishes, was laid to rest in it in 1631, the young colony began to bury its dead there. Mary Chilton, reputedly the first Pilgrim to step ashore on Plymouth Rock, is interred here with her husband. William Dawes lies nearby; this young cordwainer was the lesser known midnight rider who galloped out of Boston with Paul Revere on the night of April 18, 1775, to warn the sleeping countryside that a column of redcoats was tramping towards Concord. Close to the wall of the chapel is the tomb of Elizabeth Pain, a young Puritan woman who caught the eye of a prurient minister, bore him a child, and was branded with an "A" for her adultery. Some 200 years after her death, Nathaniel Hawthorne, preoccupied with the mystery of sin, and himself the descendant of a "grave, bearded, sable-cloaked and steeple-crowned" Puritan, celebrated her in a famous novel. She was the model for Hester Prynne in *The Scarlet Letter*.

Perhaps the most tragic of all the monuments in the Burying Ground is the cenotaph honoring the noble young Chevalier de Saint-Sauveur. He was a French naval lieutenant killed while trying to break up a street brawl between French bakers and a Boston mob. The Chevalier was visiting Boston with Count d'Estaing's fleet in 1778; and the fight erupted, it seems, when the Frenchmen refused to sell any of their crusty loaves to the citizens. (The bakery had been set up in the town to supply the fleet; the Bostonians appear to have had no flour to bake their own.) The Chevalier, *sans peur et sans reproche*, is buried in the vaults under King's Chapel.

58

EVENING TRANQUILITY AT JAMAICA POND

Jamaica Plain is a "streetcar suburb," and nobody seems at all sure how it and its pond came by the name "Jamaica." The term may commemorate Oliver Cromwell's capture of the Caribbean island in 1655, but it could just as easily refer to the partiality of 17th century Boston stevedores for a fiery slug of plain Jamaica rum. However it got its name, the ancient pond is a gem in Boston's "Emerald Necklace" of parks, and it has delighted many over the years—from British officers who skated on it before the Revolution, to urban anglers who catch its rainbow trout, and even to the strollers and joggers who tread its banks today.

Another of Boston's popular water-mounted jewels of greenery is the Charles River Esplanade, a favorite haunt of cyclists, sunbathers, Frisbee-hurlers and kiteflyers. Ever since 1929, music lovers have flocked to the Hatch Shell on the Esplanade to hear Arthur Fiedler, "Boston's Music Man," conduct the Boston Pops Orchestra. The Pops, founded in 1885, have provided a contemporary middlebrow counterpoint to the distinguished Boston Symphony Orchestra. (Center aisle seat subscriptions to the B.S.O. are passed down through generations of Brahmins as ceremoniously as family heirlooms.) Mr. Fiedler started the Esplanade concerts in order to keep music from becoming the stepchild of the rich; and in 1976 he conducted a bicentennial Fourth of July concert of the "1812 Overture" (percussion provided by howitzer cannons and fireworks) to more than 400,000 listeners. On a clear summer evening the Esplanade lawn is much more comfortable than the stuffed seats in Symphony Hall; picnicking is legal; performances are free, and usually "sold out."

BACK BAY BOTANY: EARLY BLOSSOMS ON "BOSTON'S CHAMPS ÉLYSÉES"

One hundred and fifty years ago, this balloon-bearing college student on Commonwealth Avenue could not have walked here without wading knee-deep in stinking marshland ooze. The scene is Boston's fashionable Back Bay, whose foundation was created between 1857 and 1900 from 450 acres of landfill shoveled into the tidal mud flats ("out back" of the city).

The Back Bay is laid out in the formal gridiron pattern of the French Second Empire, and has as its axis Commonwealth Avenue, whose tree-lined mall, modeled after the Parisian boulevards of Baron Haussmann, is punctuated with statuary of Boston worthies. Lewis Mumford once remarked that, with the exception of Major L'Enfant's plan for Washington D.C., Boston's Back Bay was "the outstanding achievement in American urban planning for the nineteenth century."

In this status-obsessed city, Commonwealth Avenue was said to appeal to those with plenty of money but little breeding. Residences on the sunny side of the avenue (along with those on the river side of Beacon Street) were the most prestigious. Oliver Wendell Holmes categorized his move to the Back Bay as "justifiable domicide." Henry James was not impressed. "It is all very rich and prosperous and monotonous," wrote James, "but oh, so inexpressibly vacant!"

The Victorian lamps, pictured here, straddle the entrance to the ninety-year old Algonquin Club, whose exploding magnolias each spring flush the wan face of "Comm. Ave.," as it is affectionately known to today's students. (Fraternities and junior colleges now rub shoulders with the avenue's posh condominiums and foreign consulates.)

Nearby Boylston Street, once a drab drag of seedy hotels and technical schools, now is a neon slice from a Fellini film, complete with delicatessens and karate studios, x-rated skin flicks and a Romanesque church, french crêpes and fast food, some of Boston's best sounds (at the Jazz Workshop), and its best silence (in the Boston Public Library's inner courtyard).

Wedged between Boylston and Commonwealth is Boston's youthful challenge to New York's fifth Avenue—Newbury Street, with its mono-grammed awnings, outdoor cafés, the Ritz-Carlton, Brooks Brothers, architectural styles from Gothic to art deco, chic women with ruffed poodles, elegant art galleries, imports from Alaska and Peking, and such student staples as natural food pantries, art supply stores, and chess shops.

OLD SOUTH MEETING HOUSE: THE PLACE TO BEGIN A TEA PARTY

No Boston church is richer in revolutionary lore than the Old South. John Hancock, whose flamboyant signature on the Declaration of Independence not even George III could have mistaken, delivered the annual Boston Massacre oration here in 1773. Physician and patriot, Joseph Warren, who died atop Bunker Hill, had delivered the oration the previous year, urging that "our land be a land of Liberty, the seat of virtue, the asylum of the oppressed, a name and a praise in the whole earth."

Of all its revolutionary associations, the Old South is most intimately connected with the Boston Tea Party. A mass meeting in the church, on November 29, 1773, decided that the newly-arrived tea should be returned to England without paying the King's tax or unloading it. It was from the Old South's portals on December 16 that sixty whooping "Mohawk Indians" —with blackened faces, blankets, and tomahawks—set off for Griffin's Wharf and an appointment with history.

The present church was built in 1729, to replace a cedar meeting house where Benjamin Franklin was baptized in 1706. "It was built according to the best taste of the time," an antiquarian wrote in 1876, "and forcibly recalls Sir Christopher Wren's churches."

In 1775, the British general John Burgoyne set up a riding school in the church for the 17th Light Dragoons, "overthrowing its sacred memorials and transforming it into a circus," as Boston historian Samuel Adams Drake put it. The pulpit and boxed pews were torn out and used for firewood, and the floor was strewn with cartloads of gravel. A jump bar was erected and refreshments brought in for spectators. Its usage, Drake observes, was "peculiarly malicious and repugnant."

The Old South narrowly escaped destruction in 1810 when the roof caught fire. Fortunately Isaac Harris, a fearless mastmaker, climbed to the roof and put out the flames, later receiving a handsome silver pitcher "for his intrepid and successful exhertions."

In 1876 the meeting house was sold for $1,350 in order that the land might be sold separately for $400,000. Demolition had actually begun when a preservation committee raised $400,000 and spared the building from the wrecker's hammers.

BALLOONS AT THE BUNKER HILL MONUMENT

As every street vendor knows, you can always bank on a crowd at the Bunker Hill monument on June 17, the anniversary of mighty Britain's humbling at the hands of a rag-tag army of farmers two centuries ago. Snoopy and Mickey Mouse may not exactly heighten the tone of the celebration, but many a youngster on a history tour needs to be distracted with a toy before boredom sets in. The June sun is as hot for today's children as it was for the redcoats who once toiled up the hill.

On June 17, 1775, two months after their assault on Lexington and Concord, the British chose to mount a bold frontal attack on a makeshift patriot fortification in what has become known as the Battle of Bunker Hill. (The battle, incidently was not fought on Bunker Hill at all, but on nearby Breed's Hill.) Low on ammunition, the Americans loaded their flintlocks with pebbles and nails, and were ordered by Colonel Prescott to hold their fire until they saw the "whites of their eyes." Strictly speaking, the battle was a British victory, but won at such a price as to make it indistinguishable from defeat. The "victory" cost the redcoats 1,054 casualties of their 2,450 well-groomed soldiers; their commander appears to have blundered monument-ally. "We are all wrong at the head," wrote a distraught British officer after the sanguinary action. "My mind cannot help dwelling upon our cursed mistakes....This madness or ignorance nothing can excuse." Countered patriot General Nathanael Greene after the battle, "I wish I could sell them another hill at the same price."

MUSEUM OF SCIENCE: THE DUST IS GONE

When the Museum of Science was founded in the Back Bay in 1864, it was called a "desecration of the mudflats". Today it is one of the finest of its kind in the world, and outdraws every public spectacle but the Red Sox at Fenway Park. Its original home was at the corner of Newbury and Berkeley Streets in a handsome red-brick and brownstone building (which now houses the fashionable Boston branch of Bonwit Teller).

The museum draws vitality from its new Space Age structure on the banks of the Charles. Under the directorship of Bradford Washburn, first man to climb Mt. McKinley twice (his wife was the first woman ever to reach its summit), the museum has shucked its stale and exclusive "Don't Touch" atmosphere. Children flock through its doors to play tic-tac-toe with a computer, climb aboard full-scale models of the Mercury and Apollo space capsules, gaze in wonderment at the starry heavens in the adjoining Hayden Planetarium, and gawk at the fangs of a life-size fiberglass dinosaur—a massive and ferocious Tyrannosaurus Rex. In Washburn's honorary degree citation from his alma mater, Harvard University, the museum director was described as having "moved mountains by changing a dusty Boston institution into a lively educational venture for young and old."

68

LOUISBURG SQUARE: "HUB OF THE HUB'

In the rarefied Brahmin atmosphere of Beacon Hill, Louisburg Square bestrides the city's social summit. It is here where Rolls Royces belong. Oliver Wendell Holmes called Boston the "Hub of the Universe," and Robert Lowell later dubbed Louisburg Square the "Hub of the Hub."

The elegant bow-fronted houses, dating from the early 19th century, are rich in family lore and some of the most proper Bostonians. In past years, noted residents have included Louisa May Alcott, author of "Little Women;" her father—idealist philosopher Bronson Alcott—and William Dean Howells, an editor of *Atlantic Monthly*. Jenny Lind, the "Swedish Nightingale," married her accompanist Otto Goldschmidt at No. 20 during an American tour in 1852.

At the south end of the square's lovely fenced-in park (accessible only to residents with private keys) stands a statue of Aristides the Just—the Athenian general who fought at Marathon and Salamis. A statue of Columbus stands sentinel at the north end. Both were donated by a rich Greek resident in 1849.

Today the twenty-two residents of this pinnacle of prosperity own the square outright, and still meet annually to tax themselves for its maintenance. A few pot holes are properly left in the cobblestone carriageway to slow traffic and deter would-be intruders. Outsiders who don't take this subtle hint are greeted with a less-than-hospitable sign at the entrance to this circle of antique elegance: "Trespassing cars will be towed at once."

FANEUIL HALL: "CRADLE OF LIBERTY"

The "Festung Europa" bulk of City Hall contrasts starkly with the graceful lines of distant Faneuil Hall, probably Boston's best-known building. The latter was a gift to the city from Peter Faneuil, a wealthy merchant of Huguenot stock and sybaritic tastes, who recognized the need for a market and meeting hall. It was designed by portrait painter John Smibert, and finished in 1742. Burned down in 1761, it was rebuilt on the original plan with money raised in a public lottery. Patriot James Otis appears to have dubbed it "The Cradle of Liberty" in 1763. Thereafter it rapidly became identified abroad with the Revolutionary spirit in the town.

When the Stamp Act was repealed in 1766, the town ordered Faneuil Hall to be illuminated in celebration. In 1772 a town meeting in the hall adopted Sam Adams' famous motion to appoint "a committee of correspondence...to state the rights of the colonists...as men, as Christians, and as subjects; and to communicate the same to several towns and to the world."

Redcoats slept in the hall in 1768; and, during the siege of Boston, British officers and Tory ladies staged amateur theatricals there. Charles Bulfinch added a third story and doubled the width of the elegant building in 1805, but retained its original style. Faneuil Hall is protected by charter against sale or leasing. Any group can hold meeting under its hallowed roof, and today it still echoes to some pretty revolutionary pronouncements.

ARNOLD ARBORETUM: A GEM IN THE "EMERALD NECKLACE"

At this arboretum, fall hues have tinged trees against the Boston skyline since 1872. That year James Arnold, a wealthy New Bedford merchant, established the 265-acre botanical garden as a link in the "Emerald Necklace" of Boston parks fashioned by landscape architect Frederick Law Olmsted.

While Victorian Boston did not covet New York's brash lifestyle, it did find cause to envy one of Gotham's finest possessions, lush Central Park. Boston's russet brick and wrought iron were fine to a point; but the public became worried that urban developers were gobbling up too much green space. So they called upon Olmsted—Central Park's designer—to save what was left of Boston's urban wilderness. His ingenious solution was a continuous green belt of "Emerald Necklace," which linked existing parks in Boston with planted roadways and ribbons of greenery.

The downtown Common and its smaller, more dignified botanical sister, the Public Garden, were connected to the Fenway's meadows and woodland by Commonwealth Avenue. The uptown Fens, in turn, were joined by the Riverway to Jamaicaway, Jamaica Pond, the Arnold Arboretum, and Franklin Park—which Olmsted designed in 1855. Today the arboretum contains over 6,000 different ornamental trees and shrubs from around the world, and is under the direction of Harvard University. In May and early June, its lilacs, cherry trees, forsythias, plum trees, magnolias, rhododendrons, and azaleas explode in a riot of color.

74

ROLLINS PLACE: THE "HOUSE THAT ISN'T A HOUSE'

It is said that "A city...set on a hill cannot be hid," yet one of Boston's best kept secrets is sitting atop Beacon Hill on Rollins Place. How many of "the Hill's" venerable Brahmins know what lies behind the closed green shutters at the end of this tiny cul-de-sac?

It looks like a miniature Southern mansion; swing open the wrought iron gate, stroll down the path of brick, granite and gas lamps. To your left or right you may hear, through an open window, a mesmeric minuet played on a Steinway grand, or perhaps a typewriter chattering with enough conviction to be on its fourth, possibly fifth, novel. As you approach the Greek Revival exterior, steps lead to the piazza flanked with Ionic columns and iron urns. You may imagine a Scarlett O'Hara serving high tea, or a gentleman in his housecoat perusing *The New Yorker*. A few steps closer and your imagination runs into a brick wall. This "house" isn't a house at all, but a facade masking an ugly brick-concrete wall and a twenty-foot cliff. To maintain this elegant Beacon Hill "cover-up," the neighbors on Rollins Place still hang a wreath on the porch every Christmas, plant geraniums in its urns and flowerboxes, and splash on a coat of white paint every few summers.

It's all part of the Boston tradition of saving face—architectural face. And it's not hard to keep a secret on Beacon Hill, where protocol once decreed that communication was restricted to three-way conversations between Lowells, Cabots, and God. Or perhaps the success in keeping the secret of Rollins Place has resulted from the proper Bostonian's provincial disdain for straying too far from home. As Cleveland Amory observed, "The proper Bostonian is not by nature a traveler. The Beacon Hill lady who, chided for her lack of travel, asked simply, 'Why should I travel when I'm already here?' would seem to have put the matter in a nutshell—also her compatriot who, arriving in California and asked how she came west, replied, 'Via Dedham!'"

76

A VALIANT QUAKER

The Puritans were more than devoted; they were bigoted. With an Old Testament vengeance they scourged those whose lives were less "perfect" than their own.

Boston's 17th century Puritan theocracy supplanted the Golden Rule with a golden calf of intolerance. Making a noise—or taking a walk—on the Lord's day was punishable by imprisonment in a jail which claimed the lives of half its occupants. Cursing was cured by boring through the offender's tongue with a hot iron. It was illegal for women to wear short sleeves "whereby the nakedness of the arm may be disclosed," and "silke or tiffany hoods" were forbidden unless the woman had the "visible estate" of two hundred pounds. At a time when games, theater, sports and other entertainment were outlawed, great crowds assembled to watch the hangings of more than a hundred witches, pirates, thieves and Quakers.

When two Quakers were marched to the gallows in 1759 (for breaking the law against returning from exile) they were comforted by fellow believer Mary Dyer. She, disdaining a catcalling crowd, tenderly held their hands as they trod their last earthly steps. The following year she, herself, was hanged for returning to Boston. As she went to her fate, Puritan parson John Wilson shouted, "I will carry fire in one hand and faggots in the other, to burn all Quakers in the world!" The bronze statue erected to her memory, in the shadow of the State House, acknowledges her martyrdom for religious freedom.

78

MARY DYER

QUAKER

WITNESS FOR RELIGIOUS FREEDOM

HANGED ON BOSTON COMMON 1660

"MY LIFE NOT AVAILETH ME
IN COMPARISON TO THE
LIBERTY OF THE TRUTH"

I LOVE YOU

SYLVIA SHAW JUDSON

HAYMARKET: A MOUNTAIN OF ORANGES

Stacked on pushcarts, pyramids of glossy peppers, lemons, and "Florida's finest" seem to rise to meet Boston's waterfront skyline. In this famous open-air market, the hawking tradition is older than the Revolution. Along Blackstone Street, the fruit, vegetables and meat at wholesale prices provide bargains a-plenty, even for the Beacon Hill bluebloods who come to the "people's supermarket" on Saturday mornings. They join the jostle of the hoi polloi, searching perhaps for a few choice avocadoes, crabs or camemberts. Peddlers sing out their low prices with an accent and enthusiasm that is unquestionably and delectably Italian.

A cobblestone's throw away is Boston's "Little Italy," the oldest and perhaps most colorful Boston neighborhood. Here a homey aroma of fresh sausage and baked bread wafts down Salem and Hanover Streets which are lined with white rabbits strung by their heels in butchers' windows, and barrels of dried cod, provolone and red peppers. Famous for its pastries, pasta, and bocce tournaments, the North End is also the historic home of the Old North Church and Paul Revere's House.

In front of the North End's espresso cafes on Hanover Street, new immigrants from Sicily, Rome or Naples animatedly discuss the latest soccer standings in Italy, or the forthcoming holidays honoring saints from their various towns in the Old Country. The most famous of these summer religious festivals is that of St. Anthony of Padua Da Montefalcione, whose sidewalk chapel statue is paraded once a year through narrow North End streets. Confetti falls like snow; schoolgirls, dressed like angels, are lowered by rope and pulley from upper story balconies to welcome the statue—which during the course of the day, collects a robe of dollar bill donations. These may total as much as $20,000. Indigenous or imported, traditions die hard in Boston.

COLLEGE RITES OF SPRING

In early March, winter begins to relax its hold on the city. The magnolias on Commonwealth Avenue are still a month away from bursting into bloom, but you'll find Harvard's lanky oarsmen stroking sleek red cedar racing shells up the frigid Charles River. A pair of heavyweight "eights" are pictured here against the backdrop of the nation's oldest university. The red brick building is Eliot House—named after that Brahmin dynasty which gave Harvard one of its most memorable presidents, Charles William Eliot. (It was this custodian of culture who edited that famous "five-foot shelf" of books, the "Harvard Classics".)

On the Charles River these giant water spiders glide to the clipped cadence of the coxswain's bark, the rhythmic grind of seat slides, and the gentle splash of eight oars simultaneously scooping water and leaving behind a chain of tiny whirlpools. Reveling in athletic anonymity, the crews train year round to compete in a half dozen six-minute spring races—and ultimately to realize every oarsman's dream of rowing in the Olympics or at Henley on the Thames.

No less sacred a rite of spring on the Charles is the annual measurement of Harvard Bridge in "smoots"—that marvelous unit of length invented at the Massachusetts Institute of Technology. The origin of the smoot (approximately 5 feet 9 inches) goes back to 1959 when MIT freshman Oliver Smoot joined Lambda Chi Alpha. As the story goes, his fraternity brothers put a football helmet on the rather inebriated young Smoot and rolled him head over heels the full length of Harvard Bridge, marking a red line every ten "smoots." Each year, pledges of the fraternity re-paint the stripes in a chilly pre-dawn ceremony on the bridge (which measures "exactly 364.4 smoots and an ear").

A more sober ceremony occurs in late spring. Harvard Commencement is said to be one of the last European rituals left in America, and predates presidential inaugurals by a century. A procession of top hats and ermine-trimmed academic robes begins beneath the lush elms in Harvard Yard, where each member of the faculty dutifully doffs his or her respective headgear to the statue of John Harvard, who donated his 320-volume library to the college in 1638. The black robes of the seniors cloak an air of informality, not to mention an occasional T-shirt and pair of scruffy track shoes. The uncertainty of future employment for these graduating seniors is perhaps reflected in some of their armbands which read, "You can't eat prestige."

A MAGICAL SWAN LAKE

Boston's swan boats have enchanted young and old ever since 1877, when they first glided out onto the lake in the Public Garden. Invented by "Admiral" Robert Paget, the pedal-powered paddle craft are still operated by his descendants.

Until reclaimed in 1794, the site of the Public Garden was a salt marsh. It accomodated ropeworks until 1859, when it was transformed into a delightful sylvan retreat amidst a bustling city. F. Marion Crawford, a nineteenth century romantic writer, described the Garden: "There is a smell of violets and flowers in the warm air, and down on the little pond the swan-shaped boats are paddling about with their cargoes of merry children and calico nursery maids, while the Irish boys look on from the banks and throw pebbles when the policemen are not looking, wishing they had the spare coin necessary for a ten minute voyage on the mimic sea."

In the Garden, nursemaids and mothers sit on benches instead of on the grass; and the trees, of every rank and region, are properly labeled with their botanical titles, from the Japanese Pagoda Tree (Sophora Japonica) to the Norway Maple (Acer Putanoides) and the common linden (Tilia Vulgaris).

The Public Garden is separated by Charles Street from its informal and less sophisticated neighbor, the Common—a wooded slope said to be where "bums and sailors with time heavy on their hands gravitate."

84

SORRY BETSY, THE "CONTINENTAL COLORS" CAME FIRST

You may wonder why the latter-day patriots in this Independence Day parade are bearing *not* the Stars and Stripes, but flags which incorporate the British Union Jack. These historical purists, parading across the mottled brickwork of City Hall Plaza, are flying the "Continental Colors" or "Grand Union" which was hoisted by Gen. George Washington at the Prospect Hill fortification just outside Boston on January 1, 1776.

The Continental Colors was the first flag flown by the united colonies. It bore the "King's colors" as its canton, along with the thirteen red and white stripes, because at the time colonists had not yet demanded independence but only asked for fair treatment as loyal Englishmen in the New World. The Continental Colors was the unofficial national flag at the time of the signing of the Declaration of Independence on July 4, 1776, and was used until June 14, 1777 (now celebrated as Flag Day). On that date Congress replaced the Union Jack with a blue field and thirteen white stars.

Today the Continental Colors remains largely unknown, while most of the nation embraces the legend that Betsy Ross stitched the nation's first banner. The truth of the matter is that Philadelphia's Mrs. Elizabeth (Betsy) Ross was unknown to historians until 1870 when her grandson came forward with the tale of Betsy's having met Washington and subsequently designed the first flag. But why did the public so wholeheartedly accept the patriotic story of this female upholsterer who had lost two husbands in the Revolutionary war, and sewed flags in her free time? Historians speculate that in 1870, on the eve of the nation's centennial, Americans were anxious to blot out the embarrassing memory of the Union Jack having flown on their first flag. There is no corroborating evidence in letters or diaries to confirm the story of the Betsy Ross flag with its circle of stars on a blue field; but the myth has been perpetuated through such famous paintings as Archibald Willard's "Spirit of '76," and Emanuel Leutze's "Washington Crossing the Delaware."

Nevertheless, whatever American flag is flown in Boston on the Fourth, the city seems to take an extra sense of pride. Perhaps it recalls that its truculent ways were the despair of the Mother Country a good many years before the embattled farmers "fired the shot heard 'round the world.'"

TRINITY CHURCH: RICHARDSON'S ROMANESQUE SIGNATURE IN STONE

Using good Massachusetts materials—granite from Dedham and reddish-brown freestone from Longmeadow—Henry Hobson Richardson incorporated his own bold romanticism in the design of Trinity Church in Copley Square. The original Trinity on Summer Street was ravaged in the Great Fire of 1872, and the church's rector turned to Richardson, who had flexed his architectural muscle the year before in his Romanesque design of what is now First Baptist Church in the Back Bay. (It was this church to which Frederic Auguste Bartholdi, the Franco-Italian sculptor, added a frieze of trumpeting angels, thus prompting some Bostonians to dub the edifice "The Church of the Holy Beanblowers." Bartholdi later designed the Statue of Liberty.)

Trinity was perhaps Richardson's greatest architectural achievement. The building as a whole is inspired by the southern French Romanesque style with its chunky, rock-faced stonework; but Trinity's tower is strongly influenced by Salamanca Cathedral in Spain. The entire nineteen million pound structure is supported on 4,500 wooden piles driven through the landfill which a century ago transformed the ooze of the Back Bay into dry land. Richardson, the second American to study at the École de Beaux Arts in Paris, selected John LaFarge to design the interior of the Church. Perhaps its best windows are those designed by English painter Sir Edward Burne-Jones, and fashioned by William Morris.

It was Trinity's much-loved rector, Phillips Brooks, who commissioned Richardson. Dr. Brooks became the sixth Episcopal bishop of Massachusetts in 1891, and is known throughout the English-speaking world as the author of the Christmas carol, "O Little Town of Bethlehem." Nowadays Richardson's church shares Copley Square with the monolithic sixty-story John Hancock Tower, which soars skyward at its side. The only consolation, it seems to many, is that the glass-sheeted monster reflects the genius of the Victorian architect.

THE CHRISTIAN SCIENCE CENTER: WORLD HEADQUARTERS

During Boston's Victorian "Gilded Age" religion was under attack. Nietzsche was writing God's obituary, and Darwin's "Origin of the Species" was undermining traditional faith in the Scriptures. The "Bible Commonwealth" of the founding Puritans had become a "city of conscience" as Protestants began to channel spiritual energy into social action: charities, church suppers, bazaars, reforming crusades. Rising church membership cloaked a disturbing shortage of ministers and the waning of traditional religious faith. Emerson, Thoreau, and Hawthorne, though Christian in outlook, turned their backs on church orthodoxy and began crossing ethical humanism with Transcendentalism. Bostonians flirted with spiritualism, theosophy and Eastern mysticism.

In the midst of this teeming religious reorientation, a New England woman founded a new church to "reinstate primitive Christianity and its lost element of healing." She was Mary Baker Eddy, and her concepts were—and still are—contemporary yet rooted in the teachings of Jesus. Her church flourished, and its branches and reading rooms are now to be found throught the world. Its offical name is the Church of Christ, Scientist; its teachings are Christian Science.

Healing is fundamental to this religion—healing of every kind of problem or disaster, from sickness to shyness, poverty to pollution, unhappiness to unemployment. The teachings are set out in Mrs. Eddy's textbook, *Science and Health with Key to the Scriptures*; and their application is discussed in other writings by her, and in the religious magazines and publications of her church. One of her culminating achievements was the establishment, in 1908, of *The Christian Science Monitor*, an international newspaper.

Pictured here is the white-domed Mother Church and The Christian Science Center, the religion's world headquarters. The fifteen-acre center, completed in 1975, provides a graceful interplay of old and new, and is a harmonious transition between the low-slung row houses of the Back Bay and the vertical dominance of the fifty-two-story Prudential Tower. Complementing the broad brick promenade are rows of lush lindens, rainbows of flowers, a lake-size reflecting pool, and a "dome" fountain—an environment which attracts young and old, from children in bathing suits to adults who come to read and reflect in quiet.

90

U.S.S. CONSTITUTION: "OLD IRONSIDES"

"Ay, tear her tattered ensign down!
Long has it waved on high,
And many an eye has danced to see
That banner in the sky;
Beneath it rung the battle shout,
And burst the cannon's roar;—
The meteor of the ocean air
Shall sweep the clouds no more..."

When Oliver Wendell Holmes submitted these lines to the *Boston Daily Advertiser* in 1830, he did more than pen a stirring poem about the USS Constitution. He warned a stripling nation that a treasured symbol of its new-found power and independence was slated for the breaker's yard. By rousing public indignation, he saved a doughty old warrior for posterity.

The poem has done its work well—far better, indeed, than Mr. Holmes could possibly have imagined. Not only was the *Constitution* (the oldest of the Navy's commissioned ships) rebuilt in 1833, but the public again came to its aid with funds in 1950, when its timbers were found to be rotting and the navy proposed using the vessel for target practice. Twenty years later the nation once more rallied to the forty-four-gun frigate's assistance—this time with Congressional help—and she was given a truck to keel renovation. But time continued to take its toll of her fragile fibers, and in 1973 she began a $4.4 million restoration in the Boston Navy Yard's John Quincy Adams Drydock, where she had been restored in 1833. By 1976 she had new copper sheathing and hull planking, and refurbished masts, yards, and rigging.

The *Constitution* was launched on October 21, 1797 at a cost of $302,718. In the War of 1812 she battered the British frigate *HMS Guerriere* into surrender, in a desperate battle somewhere southeast of the Gulf of St. Lawrence. It is said that shot from the British warship made so little impression on the *Constitution's* hull that an astounded tar yelled: "Huzza! Her sides are made of iron!" In December 1812 she forced *HMS Java* to haul down her colors in a brisk engagement off the coast of Brazil. Altogether she fought forty battles during her career, and never lost one.

PAUL REVERE HOUSE: NO. 19 NORTH SQUARE

Paul Revere's house, just a block away from a bustling waterfront, was almost a hundred years old when he bought it in February 1770. It cost him £213 6s. 8d. and a £160 mortgage. A rare example of English domestic architecture transplanted to the colonies, it is today the only surviving 17th century house in Boston, and it looks much as it did then. Originally the house had two and a half stories instead of the more usual one and a half; but when Paul Revere moved in with his wife, mother, and five children, it had been expanded into a three-story dwelling, with sash windows and rectangular panes.

The extra space was not to go unused. Before she died in 1773, Revere's wife, Sara, gave birth to two more daughters; and his second wife, Rachel, whom he married the same year, bore him seven more children—bringing the family's size to sixteen. Not surprisingly, the Reveres were not asked to put up British troops in 1775.

The Reveres probably moved from their crowded North Square residence after the Revolution, although the house was not sold until 1800. After Paul Revere's death in 1818, No. 19 fell into disrepair, and became a tenement and store. Fortunately it escaped the wrecker's ball, and was restored to its present state in 1908.

94